Multimedia Learning Theory

Multimedia Learning Theory

Preparing for the New Generation of Students

Edited by Patrick M. Jenlink

ROWMAN & LITTLEFIELD
Lanham • Boulder • New York • London

Published by Rowman & Littlefield
An imprint of The Rowman & Littlefield Publishing Group, Inc.
4501 Forbes Boulevard, Suite 200, Lanham, Maryland 20706
www.rowman.com

6 Tinworth Street, London SE11 5AL, United Kingdom

Copyright © 2019 by Patrick M. Jenlink

All rights reserved. No part of this book may be reproduced in any form or by any electronic or mechanical means, including information storage and retrieval systems, without written permission from the publisher, except by a reviewer who may quote passages in a review.

British Library Cataloguing in Publication Information Available

Library of Congress Cataloging-in-Publication Data Available

ISBN: 978-1-61048-848-8 (cloth : alk. paper)
ISBN: 978-1-61048-849-5 (pbk. : alk. paper)
ISBN: 978-1-61048-850-1 (electronic)

To the next generation of educators and students living in a rapidly changing digital, multimedia-infused world.

Contents

Preface		ix
Acknowledgments		xi
1	Introduction: Multimedia Learning Theory in Teaching and Learning *Patrick M. Jenlink*	1
2	Cognitive Theory of Multimedia Learning *Brooks Knight*	11
3	Multimedia Learning Theory and Its Implications for Teaching and Learning *Patrick M. Jenlink*	29
4	Multimedia Learning and the Next Generation Classroom *Patrick M. Jenlink*	43
5	The New Generation of Students *Abbey N. Boorman*	57
6	Multimedia Learning for a New Generation of Educators *Charles Lowery*	69
7	What Do Teachers and Administrators Need to Know about Multimedia Learning Theory? *Richard E. Mayer*	85
8	Next Generation Teachers: Integrating Multimedia Learning into Teacher Preparation *Patrick M. Jenlink*	109

9	Multimedia Learning and the Educational Leader *Scott McLeod*	129
10	Epilogue: The Future of Multimedia Learning in Education *Patrick M. Jenlink*	145
About the Contributors		153
About the Editor		157

Preface

As the use of digital technologies and Web 2.0 become more prevalent and the world becomes more infused with multimedia, it is important to ask to what extent, if at all, such developments change the forms and nature of knowledge. Teaching and learning in this digital, multimedia environment is increasingly challenged as the neomillennial generation enters schools and colleges having grown up with digital technologies defining their culture and shaping their cognitive and social interactions. Multimedia, for the neomillennial generation, is deeply embedded in their sensory and cognitive patterns; the neomillennials see and understand media in more sophisticated ways than their parents and the generations of society that preceded them.

The use of digital technologies is a skill set that neomillennials bring to their educational experiences, and multimedia learning has been an active pattern in shaping their understanding of communication and social interactions through various forms of social media and related technologies. Entering the public school and university classrooms requires that educators be prepared with an understanding of the neomillennial generation's culture and use of digital and multimedia in ways heretofore not experienced in educator preparation and practice.

Whether in school or college classrooms, educators will require a decidedly new paradigm of learning and teaching and wide variety of ways to stimulate the minds and cognitive development of the neomillennial generation—minds that already are working in a Web 2.0 and next-generation learning paradigm. Multimedia learning is a new paradigm that aligns with the neomillennial generation's learning needs. Drawing on representations of knowledge in more ways than text or speech, multimedia combines written and spoken text, audio, visual, graphic, and dynamic elements, such as animation and video.

This presents learners and teachers with unique resources that can be used in a wide variety of ways to stimulate various forms of learning aligned with the cognitive patterns of young minds already attuned to digital technologies and multimedia-enriched communication and sensory patterning.

Teaching and learning are complementary aspects of education. Multimedia learning consists of three key elements: instruction, which forms the "logic" of selecting, organizing, and integrating the multimedia to address the learning styles of students; content, which forms the curricular "what" of learning; and pedagogical skills, which describe the application of logic and content to specific tasks and problems, or the "how."

These three elements are mirrored in teaching by the curriculum (the "what"), the instruction (the "logic"), and the teaching pedagogy (the "how"). Multimedia digital technologies as a platform for presenting, in concert with multimedia learning theory as a theoretical foundation, affect both dimensions of teaching and learning, interfacing the teacher and learner in multiple new ways that shape the experience and culture of learning. They include how teachers engage in instructional presentations; how curriculum moves from a text-based form to a visualized-verbalized sequenced form of knowledge that is both heard and visually experienced; how students interact both *with* the sequenced medium and *through* the medium with the teacher and other learners; and how knowledge is structured within multimedia and subsequently becomes cognitive patterns in the minds of learners.

Multimedia Learning Theory: Preparing for the New Generation of Students offers a primary focus on the meaning and importance of multimedia learning theory and its application in educator preparation. Integrating multimedia learning theory into preparing the next generation of educators for their role in educating the next generation of students is presented as an important consideration for the future of our educational systems and society. Following an introduction in chapter 1, chapters 2–9 examine multimedia learning and its meaning as a theoretical foundation for next-generation learning; its implications for teaching and learning, and its influence on the classroom as a multimedia learning space; the next-generation student entering our schools and universities; multimedia learning and the next-generation teacher and educational leader. The epilogue in chapter 10 essentially presents a sense of the future direction of multimedia learning and educator preparation and practice in a world increasingly defined by multimedia and digital technologies.

Acknowledgments

The initial idea for this project began as a conversation among colleagues focused on how multimedia and digital technologies are changing the very fabric of society and how each new generation of youth increasingly is more informed by new technologies. The concern we fostered was the need to ensure that the next generation of educators is prepared to meet the learning challenges of the new generation of youth.

In our conversations, we asked what worked and what didn't work, and why. The recognition that Web 2.0 and digital technologies in concert with a growing presence of multimedia were shaping the world provoked both our concern and thinking.

Acknowledgment and thanks go to the contributing authors. Their experience in the day-to-day work of multimedia learning and digital technologies offered insight and thoughtful considerations for understanding the need for a multimedia learning perspective on educator preparation juxtaposed with the difficult struggles for advancing a concentrated focus on the invaluable role that digital technologies and multimedia learning theory play in society today.

The authors bring the welcome perspective of theorists and researchers as well as seasoned educator preparation faculty and technology experts to the discourses presented in the book. Without the contributing authors, this book would not have been possible. The authors of the chapters examining multimedia learning and educator preparation brought their considerable experience to bear on interpreting the complexity, challenges, and problems associated with reimagining educator preparation through a multimedia learning lens.

Gratitude is extended to Abbey Boorman, my doctoral intern and a contributing author of this book. Abbey's willingness to read chapters and complete citation and reference checks, as well as formatting and organization, was invaluable. Abbey has a rich knowledge of and experience with technology, which proved invaluable.

Gratitude is extended to the external reviewers who took time from their busy schedules to review and provide comments and suggestions on the chapters. Acknowledging the value of the chapters and offering constructive feedback were invaluable, as was the affirmation by reviewers for both the need and the importance of a book committed to multimedia learning theory.

Likewise, gratitude is extended to Tom Koerner and the editorial staff at Rowman & Littlefield for their vision in seeing the value of a book on multimedia learning in educator preparation that draws into specific relief the need to advance an understanding of how multimedia and digital technologies are changing society and presenting new challenges for education in public school and college classrooms and, most important, in educational preparation programs.

As well, thanks to the production staff at Rowman & Littlefield for their ever-vigilant efforts to move the book through to completion. Working with a quality publisher and the folks who turn a manuscript into a completed book is a rewarding experience.

Finally, gratitude goes to Stephen F. Austin State University for supporting this project and enabling the realization of a work that will shape educator preparation for years to come.

Chapter 1

Introduction

Multimedia Learning Theory in Teaching and Learning

Patrick M. Jenlink

Throughout the past several decades, the emergence of new media and digital technologies has been paralleled by the evolution of research and theories on cognition and learning, in particular the emergence of multimedia learning theory. As technologies have evolved, so have applications that enable the user to interface and interact with individuals locally and globally.

No generation is more at ease with media and digital technologies than today's youth entering the school and university classroom—the new millennium generation[1] who have grown up in an enriched digital technologies environment of social media and digital devices.[2] Where a traditional notebook and pen may have formed the personal choices of past generations, today's new millennium generation prefers smart phones and iPads.

The technology landscape of today, characterized by tablets, e-readers, and multimedia digital textbooks, continues to evolve and bring new opportunities for educators. The increasingly widespread adoption of tablets, mobile applications, social networks, and digital content has not only led students to expect more interaction via media and digital technology-enriched content as they learn, but it has led to the need to reconfigure both the learning environment and the preparation of educators. As such, teacher preparation needs to focus on media and digital technologies that not only provide value by motivating students to be interactive participants in learning but also increase participation, collaboration, and connections in the classroom learning environment.

With the changing face of school- and university-based learning, it is important for educators to reexamine the classroom learning environment through the lens of multimedia instruction and interaction. Integrated media instructional messages and presentations keep students engaged and improve cognitive development and learning. Multimedia integrated with digital technologies enables an advanced level of interactivity between teacher and student, and between student and student, fostering an enriched learning experience that meets the needs of diverse learners.

As such, multimedia learning theory and multimedia-based instruction in teaching and learning empower the new millennium learners and transform the learning environment of the classroom. In this chapter the author introduces the reader to the topic of multimedia learning theory and the potential and ideals it currently offers to educators and leaders in schools and universities. The author provides the reader an overview of the book's organization and content as a series of questions around multimedia learning.

MULTIMEDIA LITERACY

Teachers and instructors entering the school and university classroom today, interacting with the new millennium generation of students, will require a new level of multimedia literacy. Teaching the new millennium generation that already is skilled in the use of media and digital technologies[3] requires that teacher preparation focus on the meaning of multimedia and a familiarity with how multimedia and digital technologies are integrated into instruction and curriculum to create an immersive multimedia learning environment. The precursor to multimedia learning-embedded teaching and learning is a high level of multimedia literacy.

Multimedia literacy[4] refers to media, digital technologies, Internet, and other information and communication technologies (ICTs). Literacy in this sense includes the knowledge, skills, strategies, and dispositions required of educators to create multimedia instructional messages and presentations necessary to interacting with the new millennium generation of media and digital technologies-literate students entering the school and university classroom today. The notion of multimedia literacy transforms existing perceptions of teaching and learning into enriched, interactive, and epistemologically aligned perceptions of multimedia learning and cognition (Leu, Kinzer, Coiro, & Cammack, 2004; Miller, 2008; Tan & Guo, 2009).

Understanding the new millennium students' culture, experiences, and knowledge of the world are essential to critical and effective teaching. Embracing multimedia literacy is necessary to interacting with this generation of students pedagogically and in terms of how the students learn; using multimedia instruction requires foreknowledge of both multimedia literacy and multimedia instructional design.

The fundamental nature of a multimedia literacy approach to teacher preparation and practice, in relation to multimedia learning for the new millennium students, is that contemporary teacher preparation programs need to focus on a clear understanding of the need to reconsider preparation programs. This reconsideration is in concert with a strong multimedia-based lens of teaching and learning (Judson, 2006).

Reconsideration is inclusive of understanding that multimedia and other digital technologies themselves are forms of pedagogy. Multimedia literacy of media and digital technologies includes "the skills, strategies, and dispositions necessary to successfully use and adapt to the rapidly changing information and communication technologies and contexts that continuously emerge in . . . our professional lives" (Leu, Kinzer, Coiro, & Cammack, 2004, p. 1572). Analyzing the importance of multimedia instruction in the context of students engaged in multimedia learning activities can offer important insight into changing the teacher epistemologies as required to create a multimedia learning environment.

MULTIMEDIA LEARNING THEORY

Greer, Crutchfield, and Woods (2013) explain, "[M]ultimedia learning has its roots in the cognitive architecture that allows human learning to take place and the technological features that best support cognition" (p. 41). The origin of multimedia learning theory follows a historical path of theoretical evolution, from working memory theory (Baddeley, 1986; Baddeley & Hitch, 1974), to dual-coding theory (Paivio, 1990; Sadoski & Paivio, 2001), to cognitive load theory (Chandler & Sweller, 1991; Sweller, 1988, 1994, 2003, 2005), and to the more contemporary discussions of multimedia learning theory (Mayer, 1989a, 1989b, 1997, 2002, 2003, 2005a, 2005b; Mayer & Anderson, 1991; Mayer & Sims, 1994; Moreno & Mayer, 2007).

In a more general sense, the cognitive theory multimedia learning explains the process of learning in relation to cognition and memory. The learner has dual channels of processing new information received from multimedia messages/presentations introduced by the teacher/instructor in the learning environment (Mayer, 2005a). The dual channels are visual (nonverbal) and auditory/text (verbal), and each form of new multimedia information is processed via the learner's dual channels.

Sweller (2005) explains that there is a level of element interactivity, that is, the extent to which elements of information (both visual and auditory/verbal), as they are processed, interact. The dual channel of processing is further delineated into two forms of working memory, visual and auditory. Auditory working memory (or auditory processor) is the "component of working memory that deals with speech and other auditory information" (p. 28). Visual working memory (or visual processor) is the "component of working memory that deals visually with two- or three-dimensional objects" (p. 29).

During the introduction of the multimedia instruction message/presentation, and as the learner's brain is processing, the knowledge is introduced into working memory; that is, learning involves building mental representations of the new information (Moreno & Mayer, 2007). Sweller (2005) explains working memory as "the cognitive structure in which we consciously process information" (p. 29).

As the learner's brain processes new information, and this processed knowledge enters the working memory, it resides there for a period of time; however, as Sweller (2005) explains, the capacity and duration are limited. Knowledge that passes to long-term memory[5] is knowledge stored in the brain and from which the learner may draw for future decision making and learning.

Moreno and Mayer (2007) explain that the learner, in a multimedia learning environment, is a sense maker who works to select, organize, and integrate new information with existing knowledge. According to a knowledge construction approach to learning, the goal of instruction is to guide the learner to actively make sense of the instructional materials. Multimedia instructional messages and presentations introduce the visual (nonverbal) information using a variety of media and digital technologies in concert with the auditory/text (verbal) information to provide the learner with dual information to align with the learner's modalities of learning and cognitive patterning of information.

MULTIMEDIA LEARNING THEORY IN TEACHING

Moving beyond the traditional educational setting, where the role of the teacher is to provide the content and information to the students, through instructional media such as notes, diagrams, overhead transparencies, and models, into a multimedia learning environment, presents new challenges and demands on the teacher/instructor in school and college classrooms. The information or content presented in traditional educational settings is based on the teacher's beliefs and prescribed curriculum and other relevant information believed important to the learner.

Teaching in a school or college classroom where traditional methods and epistemological beliefs are in play is often instructor-centered, less focused on the learner and more focused on the lesson. In contrast, in the multimedia learning environment the focus is learner-centered, and instruction is designed to respond to students' needs, not just what has been set up ahead of time based on a curriculum developer's idea of who will be in the classroom or a standard curriculum mandated by external entities (Vollstädt, 2002).

Multimedia-infused instruction in teacher preparation is essential to preparing educators to enter school classrooms and transform the learning environment into one that through multimedia stresses the role of students; that is, it is learner-centered, and multimedia accentuates the importance of interactivity between teacher and student as well as between student and student (Yang & Fang, 2008). An important feature of multimedia teacher preparation and practice is to use multimedia instruction to improve learners' ability to listen and speak, and to develop their communicative competence. Using multimedia in the context of creation of multimedia learning environments ensures a viable context for the exchange between teachers and students.

Changing the focus of teaching and learning to a multimedia-based, learner-centered approach will require that universities change teacher preparation programs and instructional practices to integrate multimedia and digital technologies and multimedia learning theory into the epistemological and pedagogical architecture of educator preparation. Multimedia learning brings to the foreground an integrated, interactive, multisensory approach to preparation and practice that more clearly aligns with the new millennium generation of students entering the school and university classroom.

QUESTIONS TO ASK CONCERNING MULTIMEDIA LEARNING

The questions that universities and educator preparation programs need to ask in preparation for evolving to multimedia and digital technologies-enhanced programs are many. First, what is multimedia learning theory, and how do we integrate it into our current way of teaching and learning? This will be a difficult but important step forward into rethinking educator preparation and ultimately the practice of teachers in school classrooms.

Second, what are the implications of multimedia learning theory for teaching and learning, both at the school and university level, and for the future generation of students entering classrooms? As the implications are examined and the reality of exactly what will need to change, in terms of teaching and learning, and how the change will affect education and educators in the long term may well be frightening. Yet, the change is critically needed if education and educators alike are to meet the needs of the new millennium generation entering the school and university. Implications are varied, including implications for how to prepare educators, approach instruction and curriculum with/through multimedia, engage the learner cognitively, and work with new technologies to transform teaching and learning in the school and university, and in society at large.

Third, what will the multimedia classroom look like, and what changes will we need to undergo in education and in the public to ensure that the change is clearly supported and embraced? The classroom of today will not exist, nor will the models of instruction and design, curriculum, and learning as we know them or have experienced them until now. Integrating multimedia learning theory and the requisite multimedia and digital technologies will require a complete rethinking of how learning space and human interaction function; rethinking in relation to the teacher as multimedia learning instructional designer and facilitator and the student as interactive, participatory, digital technology savvy, and multimedia-engaged learner.

Fourth, what is the new generation of youth entering schools and universities, and how do they differ from the past generation? The importance of this questions lies, in large part, with understanding how the new millennium generation is different. Equally important is examining society's role, along with the role of parents and guardians, in relation to how the infusion of media and digital technologies has shaped learning needs along with cognitive development of learners. A generation that has grown up with increasing access to technologies and media experiences will present new challenges in the school and university classroom. How the new generation receives and engages in the experiences of the classroom is equally important.

Fifth, what are the learning and cognitive needs of the new millennium generation entering classrooms, and how will educators align with an already multimedia- and digital technologies-literate population? The new millennium generation is extremely adept at the use of multimedia and digital technologies, well beyond the level of the older generation currently working in educational settings, both school and university. The challenge is to recognize the level of sophistication and literacy of the new millennium generation and draw on its strength to give direction to revising educator preparation and practice.

Sixth and last, what does the future hold for education as the technological universe continues to expand and evolve at an exponential rate that is unprecedented in today's world and portends to do so much more in coming years? Education and those who enter schools and universities to take active roles in teaching and learning of the new millennium generation will need to embrace the advancements in media and digital technologies, realizing that the current rate of technological innovation is changing the fabric of society.

That said, education as it existed in the previous century and as it exists today will never be what it was or is as society and technologies continually evolve. Rather, it will require each new generation of educators to adapt and evolve in concert with society and the technologies that continue to enable communication to evolve and the demand for new vistas of teaching and learning attentive to the way that the new millennium generation, and the generations that come next, need in order to learn successfully.

CONCLUSION

Currently, our approaches to educator preparation and practice, as related to preparing contents and delivering learning materials, need to evolve according to the existence of multimedia and digital technologies currently guiding society. This means that multimedia literacy is of critical important in preparing next-generation teachers for the new millennium students entering the classroom. Equally important, this means that multimedia learning theory as a guide to pedagogical and epistemological understanding is critically important in preparing the next generation of educators.

The school and university classroom can no longer be a static physical space with predetermined arrangements of desks and students, but rather a dynamic space that enables interactivity in learning. Whether in the school or college classroom, educators need a level of literacy and understanding of multimedia learning theory required to integrate multimedia and digital technologies into their process of teaching and learning.

They will need to rethink the epistemological and pedagogical orientations we currently use in understanding teaching and learning, in particular the learning theories that inform how we approach teaching and learning. Equally important, we will need to reconfigure our understanding of the relationship of instructor to student as well as the relationship of instructional delivery of content to the learning modalities and cognitive preferences of the learner. As multimedia and digital technologies continue to evolve in society, so will the need for the evolution in how we define and practice teaching and learning in media- and digital technologies-infused global society.

NOTES

1. Various metaphors describe the new generation of students entering schools and universities, including Digital, Millennial, Gen X, and Gen Y. For purposes of this chapter, the metaphor new millennium will be used. The new millennium student shows differences between students within the age range of students thought to form a single generation. These differences are most marked in relation to the newer media, technologies, and social networking sites (Ananiadou, 2010; Ferris, 2012; Jones & Shao, 2011).

2. Society also has seen a rise in the use of social media applications such as Facebook, Twitter, Instagram, Skype, Zoom, Flickr, and Blogs among the new millennium generation, but it is unclear the extent to which the academic world embraces these applications (Clarke, 2012; Howe & Strauss, 2000; Neo, T.-K., Neo, J., & Kwok, J. W., 2009).

3. Buckingham (2007) explained that different media literacies—that is, literacies required for smart phone, Facebook, iPad, and others—are acquired by individuals through their use of media and digital technologies. With this in mind, the new millennium generation of students entering classrooms today has an evolved level of media literacies. Multimedia literacy is quintessential to successful teaching and learning in school and university classrooms. Multimedia learning requires multimedia literacies as both critical and creative factors in teaching and learning. The metaphor of multimedia literacy provides a means of imagining a more coherent and ambitious approach to teaching and learning, and the requisite preparation required for the educator entering classrooms today.

4. Multimedia literacy speaks to the multimodal nature of learning and cognition. Lotherington and Jenson (2011) explain: "Multimodal literacies transcend the alphabetic world that is the focus of classroom literacy instruction. A generation ago, the world of literacy was based on paper. Now, literacy engages people in texts and discourses that traverse space and time on screens in which we can access and mix semiotic resources that include a multiplicity of languages. We do this instantaneously and ubiquitously, using new media in constant evolution" (p. 226).

5. Sweller (2005) explains that long-term memory is "the cognitive structure that stores our knowledge base. We are only conscious of those contents of long-term memory that are transferred to working memory" (p. 29). Drawing long-term memory into working memory occurs when the learner is processing new information.

REFERENCES

Ananiadou, K. (2010). *New millennium learners: Evidence and educational implications of learners' attachment to digital media and connectedness.* Retrieved from www.oecd.org/edu/nml.

Baddeley, A. (1986). *Working memory.* New York, NY: Oxford University Press.

Baddeley, A., & Hitch, G. (1974). Working memory. In G. A. Bower (Ed.), *Recent advances in learning and motivation* (Vol. 8, pp. 47–89). New York: Academic Press.

Buckingham, D. (2007). *Schooling the digital generation: Popular culture, new media and the future of education.* London, UK: UCL IOE Press.

Chandler, P., & Sweller, J. (1991). Cognitive load theory and the format of instruction. *Cognition and Instruction, 8*(4), 293–332. doi:10.1207/s1532690xci0804_2.

Clarke, R. Y. (2012). *The next-generation classroom: Smart, interactive and connected learning environments.* White paper sponsored by Samsung. Alexandria, VA: IDC Government Insights.

Ferris, S. P. (2012). *Teaching, learning and the net generation: Concepts and tools for teaching digital learners*. Hershey, PA: IGI Global.

Greer, D. L., Crutchfield, S. A., & Woods, K. L. (2013). Cognitive theory of multimedia learning, Instructional design principles, and students with learning disabilities in computer-based and online learning environments. *Technology in Education, 193*(2), 41–50.

Howe, N., & Strauss, B. (2000). *Millennials rising: The next great generation*. New York, NY: Vintage Books.

Jones, C., & Shao, B. (2011). *The net generation and digital natives: Implications for higher education*. York, UK: Higher Education Academy.

Judson, E. (2006). How teachers integrate technology and their beliefs about learning: Is there a connection? *Journal of Technology and Teacher Education, 14*(3), 581–597.

Leu, D. J., Jr., Kinzer, C. K., Coiro, J. L., & Cammack, D. W. (2004). Towards a theory of new literacies emerging from the Internet and other information and communication technologies. In R. B. Ruddell & N. J. Unrau (Eds.), *Theoretical models and processes of reading* (5th ed., pp. 1570–1613). Newark, DE: International Reading Association.

Lotherington, H., & Jenson, J. (2011). Teaching multimodal and digital literacy in L2 settings: New literacies, new basics, new pedagogies. *Annual Review of Applied Linguistics, 31*, 226–246.

Mayer, R. E. (1989a). Models for understanding. *Review of Educational Research, 59*, 43–64.

Mayer, R. E. (1989b). Systematic thinking fostered by illustrations in scientific text. *Journal of Educational Psychology, 81*, 240–246.

Mayer, R. E. (1997). Multimedia learning: Are we asking the right questions? *Educational Psychologist, 32*, 1–19.

Mayer, R. E. (2002). Cognitive theory and the design of multimedia instruction: An example of the two-way street between cognition and instruction. *New Directions for Teaching and Learning, 89*, 55–71.

Mayer, R. E. (2003). The promise of multimedia learning: Using the same instructional design methods across different media. *Learning and Instruction, 12*, 125–139.

Mayer, R. E. (2005a). Cognitive theory of multimedia learning. In R. E. Mayer (Ed.), *The Cambridge handbook of multimedia learning* (pp. 31–48). Cambridge, UK: Cambridge University Press.

Mayer, R. E. (2005b). Principles for managing essential processing multimedia learning: Segmenting, pretraining, and modality principles. In R. E. Mayer (Ed.), *Cambridge handbook of multimedia learning* (pp. 169–182). New York, NY: Cambridge University Press.

Mayer, R. E., & Anderson, R. B. (1991). Animations need narrations: An experimental test of a dual-coding hypothesis. *Journal of Educational Psychology, 83*, 484–490.

Mayer, R. E., & Sims, V. K. (1994). For whom is a picture worth a thousand words? Extensions of a dual-coding theory of multimedia learning. *Journal of Educational Psychology, 86*(3), 389–401.

Miller, S. M. (2008). Teacher learning for new times: Repurposing new multimodal literacies and digital-video composing for schools. In J. Flood, S. B. Heath, & D. Lapp (Eds.), *Handbook of research on teaching literacy through the communicative and visual arts* (Vol. 2, pp. 441–460). Newark, DE: International Reading Association; New York, NY: Taylor & Francis.

Moreno, R., & Mayer, R. (2007). Interactive multimodal learning environments. *Educational Psychology Review, 19*, 309–326. doi:10.1007/s10648-007-9047-2.

Neo, T.-K., Neo, M., & Kwok, J. W. J. (2009). Engaging students in a multimedia cooperative learning environment: A Malaysian experience. In *Same places, different spaces*. Proceedings ASCILITE Auckland 2009. Retrieved from http://www.ascilite.org.au/conferences/auckland09/procs/neo.pdf.

Paivio, A. (1990). *Mental representations: A dual coding approach*. New York, NY: Oxford University Press.

Sadoski, M., & Paivio, A. (2001). *Imagery and text: A dual coding theory of reading and writing*. Mahwah, NJ: Erlbaum.

Sweller, J. (1988). Cognitive load during problem solving: Effects on learning. *Cognitive Science, 12*, 257–285.

Sweller, J. (1994). Cognitive load theory, learning difficulty, and instructional design. *Learning and Instruction, 4*(4), 295–312.

Sweller, J. (2003). Evolution of human cognitive architecture. In B. H. Ross (Ed.), *The psychology of learning and motivation* (vol. 43, pp. 215–266). New York, NY: Academic Press.

Sweller, J. (2005). Implications of cognitive load theory for multimedia learning. In R. E. Mayer (Ed.), *The Cambridge handbook of multimedia learning* (pp. 19–30). Cambridge, UK: Cambridge University Press.

Tan, L., & Guo, L. (2009). From print to critical multimedia literacy: One teacher's foray into new literacies practices. *Journal of Adolescent & Adult Literacy, 53*(4), 315–324.

Vollstädt, W. (2002). *Zukünftige Entwicklung von Lehrund Lernmedien: Ausgewählte Ergebnisse einer Delphi-Studie*. Cornelsen Stiftung, Berlin. Papers from the Neue Medien und Schulentwicklung Symposium, 25. University of Bielefeld.

Yang, W., & Fang, F. (2008). Optimization of multimedia English teaching in context creation. *International Education Studies, 1*(4), 136–142.

Chapter 2

Cognitive Theory of Multimedia Learning

Brooks Knight

INTRODUCTION

Advances in and increased educational integration of technology establish theory and contemplation concerning validity and potential of technology in the educational setting. Copious questions emerge about adequate procedures to achieve excellence in student achievement and learning. One inquiry regards mental refinement of information mapping as opposed to mental connections. When considering newly acquired intellectual property, multimedia learning is less about mental cartography and more akin to the connections of national alliances.

In his forward to the book *The Three-Pound Universe*, written by Hooper and Teresi, Isaac Asimov (1986) wrote, "The human brain, then, is the most complicated organization of matter that we know" (pp. xiii–xvi). He was referring to the complicated physical matter organization in which the brain is formed, but alternately, the analogy can be used to illustrate the brain as the most complicated organizer of information that matters to humans.

Researching and understanding cognition is of paramount importance to a species that hopes to better understand its thinking and facilitate learning. The cognitive theory of multimedia learning provides insight into student cognition and is assembled around three cognitive processes and five principles that explicate the brain's ability to organize and evolve connections.

COGNITIVE PROCESSES

The first cognitive process, *selecting*, is the moment of cognition when an individual participates in an activity that involves both auditory and visual components. During this initial process, the individual yields a text base, conceived from verbal information, and an image base, conceived from the visual information. With these bases—text and image—the second cognitive process, *organizing*, begins. The organization process involves mentally creating, as Mayer and Moreno (1998) describe, a "verbally-based model of the to-be-explained system," which is then applied to the image base to create the "visually-based model" (p. 2). Once the verbal and visual bases have been established within the individual, the final cognitive process, *integrating*, begins. The integration involves using the verbal and visual base to render connections between the two as the mind creates a structure to solidify understanding and prepare future application. This can be summarized in Mayer's (2005) words: "People learn more deeply from words and pictures than from words alone" (p. 3).

PRINCIPLES OF MULTIMEDIA LEARNING THEORY

The research-based principles presented to support the multimedia learning theory find strength in similar simple fashion. In response to the nature of the principles, they are in three groups. First are major principles of how to use multimedia to aid students' comprehension of a scientific explanation, followed by additional basic supportive principles, and finally advanced supportive principles.

Mayer (1997) defines the multiple representation principle: "it is better to present an explanation in words and pictures than solely in words" (p. 2). This represents the notion that having video is more beneficial than not having it or, more explicitly, that "using two modes of representation rather than one" establishes improved understanding and memory retention (p. 2).

The *contiguity* principle states, "[W]hen giving a multimedia explanation, present corresponding words and pictures contiguously rather than separately" (Mayer, 1997, p. 3). This simultaneous presentation creates increased student understanding by stimulating mental structures established by the verbal and visual cognitive bases. The *split-attention* principle states, "[W]hen giving a multimedia explanation, present words as auditory narration rather than as visual on-screen text" (p. 3). This further establishes increased sensory attention that improves learning.

Ayres and Sweller (2005) when defining split-attention state, "[I]nstructional split-attention occurs when learners are required to split their attention between and mentally integrate several sources of physically or temporally disparate information" (p. 135). Text, being presented auditorily rather than visually, in tandem with multimedia allows increased connections by not monopolizing mental focus on single forms of stimulation, thereby inherently establishing sensory and intellectual conjunction.

The *individual differences* principle is established by Mayer (1997): "[T]he foregoing principles are more important for low-knowledge than high-knowledge learners and for high-spatial rather than low-spatial learners" (p. 4). This clearly states that increased levels of ignorance are affected more by the multimedia affect; in addition, students' ability to hold visual images in the visual working memory for extended periods increases their benefit from contiguous presentation of words and pictures. The ignorance of material accords the student an increased potential spectrum of understanding, as they are not muddled by previous mental images.

Moreover, the *coherence* principle posits that conciseness is preferable by stating that "when giving a multimedia explanation, use few rather than many extraneous words and pictures" (Mayer, 1997, p. 4). A coherent summary, which highlights relevant words and pictures, has an improved effect on multimedia learning compared to a longer one. Mayer's theory presents the belief that the brain selects and organizes words and pictures to create mental constructs, discounting that these elements are dichotomous in mental processing.

Additional basic principles are a foundation for the theory of multimedia learning. The *multimedia principle* states, "[P]eople learn better from words and pictures than from words alone" (Fletcher & Tobias, 2005). Mayer (2006) explains this more specifically: people learn more deeply when appropriate pictures are combined with the text. It is established, however, that pictures are not ubiquitously advantageous in identical manners. It is in response to children's learning evolution that their books shift to fewer and fewer pictures over time.

This shifting away from visual information supports the Tobias (1989) hypothesis related to the individual differences principle, which upon research found "students high in general ability tended to succeed with instruction that offered little assistance, whereas students of less ability profited when various forms of assistance were added" (p. 1). The overarching intent of the multimedia principle does not imply a lack of variances in improved learning, the simple argument being that learning is improved when pictures are available to enhance text.

The *modality principle* begins with evidence indicating that the manner in which information is presented affects how well it is retained and learned (Mayer, Bove, Bryman, Mars, & Tapangco, 1996). Low and Sweller (2005), referring to the modality principle, state, "[I]nformation presented in a mixed mode (partly visual and partly auditory) is more effective than when the same information is presented in a single mode (either visual or auditory alone)" (p. 147).

Next, Low and Sweller (2005) explain that people learn better from graphics and narration than graphics and printed text: "Students learn better when the associated statements are narrated rather than presented visually" (p. 147). During the multimedia learning theory cognitive process of *selecting*, the modality principle establishes that increased mental retention is available when the auditory senses are involved. This is an enhancement to the multimedia learning theory, advancing the establishment of improved learning through multiple modes of presentation.

The *redundancy principle* (Sweller, 2005) states, "[R]edundant material interferes with rather than facilitates learning," and people learn better when the same information is not presented in more than one format (p. 159). An explanation of the redundancy principle using cognitive load theory suggests,"[C]oordinating redundant information with essential information increases working memory load, which interferes with the transfer of information to long-term memory" (p. 159). This supports the coherence theory by establishing that simplicity in presentation has paramount importance for retention by learners.

Also important, the *segmenting, pretraining,* and *modality principles* (Mayer, 2005) state that people learn better when a multimedia message is presented in learned-paced segments rather than as a continuous unit, they learn better from a multimedia message when they know the names and characteristics of the main concepts, and they learn better from a multimedia message when the words are spoken rather than written. Mayer (2005) continues by stating, "[S]egmenting gives the learners the time they need to carry out essential processing" while "pretraining reduces the amount of essential processing that is required" (p. 170).

In addition, the *personalization, voice and image principles* (Mayer, 2005) state that people learn better when the words of a multimedia presentation are in conversational style rather than formal style and when the words are spoken in a standard-accented human voice rather than a machine voice or foreign-accented voice; but people do not necessarily learn better when the speaker's image is on the screen (p. 201).

Finally, a set of advanced principles reinforces the theory of multimedia learning. The set includes nine principles, which are not necessarily sequential in nature:

- First, the *guided-discovery principle* (de Jong, 2005, p. 216) states that people learn better when guidance is incorporated into discovery-based multimedia environments.
- Second, the *worked-out example principle* (Renkl, 2005, p. 230) demonstrates that people learn better when they receive worked-out examples in initial skill learning.

- Third, the *collaboration principle* (Jonassen, Lee, Yang, & Laffey, 2005, p. 247) states that people can learn better with collaborative online learning activities.
- Fourth, the *self-explanation principle* (Roy & Chi, 2005, p. 272) states that people learn better when they are encouraged to generate self-explanations during learning.
- Fifth, the *animation* and *interactivity principles* (Betrancourt, 2005, p. 287) state that people do not necessarily learn better from animation than from static diagrams.
- Sixth, the *navigation principles* (Rouet & Pottelle, 2005, p. 297) state that people learn better in hypertext environments when appropriate navigation aids are provided.
- Seventh, the *site map principle* (Shapiro, 2005, p. 313) states that people can learn better in an online environment when the interface includes a map showing where the learner is in the lesson.
- Eighth, the *prior knowledge principle* (Kalyuga, 2005, p. 325) states that instructional design principles that enhance multimedia learning for novices may hinder multimedia learning for more expert learners.
- Ninth, the *cognitive aging principle* (Paas, Van Gerven, & Tabbers, 2005, p. 339) explains that instructional design principles that effectively expand working memory capacity are especially helpful for older learners.

DUAL-CODING THEORY AND COGNITIVE LOAD

The multimedia learning theory assumes that two separate channels, auditory and visual, process information. This has been referred to as dual-coding theory (DCT), which evolved from specific experiments on the role of imagery in associate learning (Paivio, 1963, 1965, 1991). Clark and Paivio (1991) suggest with the dual-coding theory that information received by the brain is coded for retrieval according to the modality in which it is received.

This theory suggests that when mentally coding, "theoretically distinct verbal and nonverbal symbolic modes" are rendered (Clark & Paivio, 1991, p. 151). The verbal mode is distinguished by "word-like representations which are "modality specific" while the nonverbal mode establishes "modality specific images for . . . nonlinguistic objects and events" (p. 151). Also assumed is that each channel has a limited, or finite, capacity. This is similar to a notion of cognitive load, which suggests that learning is best achieved during conditions aligned with human cognitive architecture (Sweller, 1988, 1999).

An assumption that also predicts the success of multimedia learning by default is that learning is an active process of filtering, selecting, organizing, and integrating information based on prior knowledge. This is fully reflected in the cognitive processes established by Mayer (1997, 2005). Another assumption Mayer (1997) acknowledges regards that the bulk of instructional presentation resides as verbal. This reflects the standard for all communication in an educational setting but does not constitute capacity for human information processing. The multimedia learning theory posits that multimedia presentation represents a comprehensive approach to accommodate the human information processing capacity.

DEFINING THE THEORY

One ubiquitously accepted definition of multimedia does not exist, but, as shown by the following, the variances are not spread across a large spectrum. Multimedia is described by various researchers as the "use of multiple forms of media in a presentation" (Schwartz & Beichner, 1999, p. 8); the "combined use of several media, such as movies, slides, music, and lighting" (Brooks, 1997, p. 17); "information in the form of graphics, audio, video, or movies. A multimedia document contains a media element other than plain text" (Greenlaw & Hepp, 1999, p. 44); and "presenting both words (such as spoken text or printed text) and pictures (such as illustrations, photos, animation, or video)" (Mayer, 2005, p. 2).

By words, Mayer (2005) is describing material presented in verbal form. By pictures, he means any material presented in pictorial form. The goal of the theory, as Mayer (2005) states, is to determine "how people learn from words and pictures, and how to design multimedia learning environments that promote learning" (p. 1). This establishes the continued process by scholars to surpass mere acknowledgment that pictures and video enhance learning when combined with text but continue to research methods in which multimedia learning can advance educational connections within the mind of the student.

DEVELOPMENT OF THE THEORY

Mayer has based the majority of his multimedia work on an integration of Sweller's cognitive load theory (Chandler & Sweller, 1991; Sweller, 1999), Paivio's dual-coding theory (Clark & Paivio, 1991; Paivio, 1986), and Baddeley's working memory model (1986, 1992, 1999). Sweller's cognitive load theory suggests, "[E]ffective instructional material facilitates learning by directing cognitive resources towards activities that are relevant to learning rather than toward preliminaries to learning" (Chandler & Sweller, 1991, p. 293).

Mayer and Moreno (2003), concerned with cognitive overload in which the learner's intended cognitive processing exceeds the learner's available cognitive capacity, wrote *Nine Ways to Reduce Cognitive Load in Multimedia Learning*. The influence of the cognitive load theory on multimedia learning is never more noticeable than when Mayer and Moreno (2003) refer to cognitive load as the "central consideration in the design of multimedia instruction" (p. 43).

Paivio's dual-coding theory has its roots in the practical use of imagery as a memory aid 2,500 years ago (Yates, 1966). As Paivio (1991) writes, the "memory emphasis evolved into broader applications of imagery aimed at accelerating the acquisition of knowledge" (p. 149). Consistent with this theory, Mayer and Sims (1994) write,

> Spatial ability allows high-spatial learners to devote more cognitive resources to building *referential connections* between visual and verbal presentations of presented material . . . low-spatial ability learners must devote more cognitive resources to building *representation connections* between visually presented material and its visual representation. (p. 389)

The obvious connection to multimedia learning is the direct correlation to the *individual differences* principle. According to this principle, imagery has greater impact for low-knowledge, high-spatial learners.

Working memory (Baddeley, 1992) refers to "a brain system that provides temporary storage and manipulation of the information necessary for such complex cognitive tasks as language comprehension, learning, and reasoning" (p. 556). In a study to identify techniques for presentation of verbal and pictorial information that minimizes working-memory load, Mayer and Moreno (1998) provide an example of how studying multimedia learning environments "can lead to advances in basic cognitive theory" (p. 319).

The concern also is about how to characterize a form of presentation if it involves more than one form of multimedia. The three solutions to this are the delivery media view, the presentation modes view, and the sensory modalities view. According to Mayer (2005), the "delivery media . . . requires two or more delivery devices . . . the presentation modes view, multimedia requires verbal and pictorial representations . . . the sensory modalities view, multimedia requires auditory and visual senses" (p. 2).

Mayer (2005) rejects the media view due to the focus on technology rather than the learner. Mayer instead opts for the presentation modes view and, to a smaller extent, the sensory modalities view. Mayer (2005) states that the presentation modes view "allows for a clear definition of multimedia . . . and is commonly used by multimedia researchers" (p. 2).

The presentation modes view is also the basis for Paivio's (1986) dual-coding theory, on which Mayer based some of his multimedia work. The rationale for the study of multimedia learning, as Mayer (2005) states, is "that students may learn more deeply from words and pictures than from words alone . . . what is needed is a research-based understanding of how people learn from words and pictures and how to design multimedia instruction that promotes learning" (pp. 5–6).

VALIDATION OF THE THEORY

As Hyde and Jenkins (1973) established, repetition alone in learning will not suffice. Their research also clarified that wanting to remember was not a determining factor. As Willingham (2009) states, "[H]ow marvelous it would be if memory did work this way. Students would sit down with a book, say to themselves, 'I want to remember this,' and they would!" (p. 46). Without the ability to depend solely on the metaphorical heart and passion of the student to establish his structure and strength for learning, the association the human mind renders deserves ubiquitous concentration.

On this topic, Mayer (1997) states that research had "produced convincing evidence that presenting a verbal explanation of how a system works does not insure that students will understand the explanation" (p. 1). In Mayer's eight studies at the University of California regarding the "presentation of computer-generated animations synchronized with computer-generated narration or presenting illustrations next to corresponding text," there were three points of consistent evidence for the multimedia effect (p. 1). In these studies,

> Students received coordinated presentation of explanations in verbal and visual format (multiple representation group), their median rendered 75 percent more creative solutions on problem-solving transfer tests than did students who received verbal explanations alone . . . Students rendered a median of over 50 percent more creative solutions to transfer problems when verbal and visual explanations were coordinated (integrated group) than when they were not coordinated (separated group). (Mayer, 1997, p. 1)

In the same studies, Mayer (2007) established, "[M]ultimedia and contiguity effects were strongest for low prior knowledge and high spatial ability students" (p. 1).

RELEVANCE TO DEMOGRAPHICS

Multimedia learning is useful for varied cultures and races (Inkpen, 1997; Passig & Levin, 1999). The multimedia learning effect has shown to have a relatively uniform effect on participants (Mayer, 1996). The multimedia learning effect is independent of race or gender. Certainly, the use of the internet and computers does not establish directly the validity of a multimedia learning theory. However, the increased usage across the planet can be deemed as information worthy of influence when considering a new consciousness of thinking and curriculum.

By 2005, 19.9 percent of children ages three to four and 20.1 percent of people ages seventy or older were accessing the internet on a regular basis (NCES, 2005). These represented the lowest percentages; ages fifteen to nineteen represented the highest at 77.7 percent (NCES, 2005). In the same year, 73.4 percent of caucasions, 53 percent of African Americans, and 34.9 percent of Hispanics regularly used the internet (NCES, 2005).

In addition, 64.6 percent of males and 67.6 percent of females had internet activity (NCES, 2005). Given this, the concept can be universally explained and applied in education. The global network and marketplace have created connections between individuals living thousands of miles apart, and with current technology offering face-to-face interaction to the masses, the opportunity has increased for mental stimulation by multimedia lessons.

Internet World Stats (2011) reported in March 2011 that the internet had more than 2 billion users worldwide. Asia represented the greatest percentage at 44 percent; Europe, 22.7 percent; and North America, 13 percent. The global impact of the internet also transitions to schools in the United States. In schools, percentages were displayed by the National Center for Education Statistics (NCES). Internet access rose from 8 percent in 1995 to 94 percent in 2005 and is in virtually all now (National Center for Educational Statistics, 2010).

The ratio of students to instructional computers with internet access was 6 to 1 in 2000. By 2005, the number had dropped to 3.8 and by 2008 to 3.1 (NCES, 2010). The national information infrastructure provides students with opportunities to research, connect abroad, and learn in a multimedia setting.

In the Fall of 2008, 97 percent of school districts reported having a local area network, and 100 percent reported having internet access (NCES, 2009). A student no longer is limited to reading a book or article about the war in Darfur, hoping a single picture will create the imagery necessary to illustrate the war's magnitude. A student from Darfur can give his counterpart information directly about how Darfur is changing while simultaneously projecting relevant video and pictures. Schools are increasingly embracing this face-to-face connection. Teamed with a local network, students are increasingly prepared for life after school.

The local area network allows a student to access the internet, maintain his files on a localized server, and manage a login that links all of his network activity to his name. This empowers the school to oversee usage by students and to access and recognize trends in learning while maintaining an acceptable use policy. The ability of the students, faculty, and staff to save documents and other files to a daily backed-up centralized location offers increased dependability and ease of use. In addition to keeping data, servers provide the opportunity for teachers to organize lesson plans, videos, and Web pages.

The same NCES (2009) report stated that 82 percent of elementary and 83 percent of secondary schools offered server space for posting their own Web pages or class materials (NCES, 2009). The Web pages are an opportunity for the teacher to express ideals, provide classroom information, and accommodate multimedia learning through interactive pictures, sound, and text.

Beyond the classroom, the community is becoming increasingly connected. The United States Census Bureau (2010) reported that in 2003, 61.8 percent of households had a computer and 54.7 percent had internet access. Beginning in 2007, respondents were not asked questions about computer ownership. In the same report, 68.7 percent of homes had internet access in 2009. To project out the percentage of homes with computers, based on the increase in internet access, 77.6 percent of homes had computers in 2009.

Educational purposes are not the universal rationale when purchasing a computer; the multimedia effect is displayed in full glory as millions each day spend hours perusing for new clothes, debating political issues, and watching videos of dancing dogs. These are all embraced in large part due to the increased ability of the brain to process new information from the pictures and video combined with text.

It would be hard to consider individuals buying clothes without a picture to support what is written about it, or to enjoy and distribute the story of a Chihuahua dancing the salsa in plain text. However, it is not labeled as education because it lacks intrinsic value for schools. This does not discount the magnitude of importance regarding the shift in minds about which ways information is best digested.

Technology is also affecting the treatment of preventable diseases that kill millions yearly. Larkin (2006) stated, "[F]ew Americans understand that global health may be one of the most important issues of this century and that in today's borderless society our health is inextricably bound to others" (p. 18). The medical field and medical education are strengthened by hands-on experience. Medical students will dissect a human cadaver as freshmen (Bergeron, 2005). Some medical schools place their students in the field immediately (Isger, 2011). The obvious connection to multimedia theory regards the importance of a visual and, of course, hands-on approach to learning.

The captivating nature and popularity of the network connection created by social networking and information availability inevitably provide new opportunities for discourse and learning regardless of diversity. Facebook reaches 56 percent of the active U.S. internet universe with an average usage of six hours a month per user, and it is the third most-visited site by users 65 and older (Gyimesi, 2009). The revolution in Egypt was in large part due to the impact that social media possesses (Smith, 2011). The impact of the internet is obvious, and underlying it is the importance of multimedia in human connection to learning, evolution, and progression.

USE AND APPLICATION OF THE THEORY

Wanting to remember and wanting to learn do not translate into remembering or learning, or, as Hyde and Jenkins (1973) established, the "intention-to-learn dimension produced very little difference in either recall or associative structure" (p. 472). This demands new ideas in education from designers of new curriculum, which do not offer the student a choice in the matter. The multimedia learning theory is beneficial to all creators of curriculum as they embrace a new generation of learners and learning styles.

Previously, a classroom could merely offer the opportunity for a teacher to read aloud as the students followed, processing each word and picture on their own. The increased opportunity new technology provides in the classroom for student pacing and multimedia influence allows teachers, curriculum creators, and all others with influence on learning to integrate multimedia theory into current capabilities. In addition, this theory applies across all subjects, as the mind can learn geometry from spatial connections in video and an hour later create understanding of a Dickensian character's life through pictures and audio.

CRITIQUES OF THE THEORY

Multimedia learning theory avoids one critique of media comparison (Lockee, Burton, & Cross, 1999) by establishing an investigative perspective of multimedia, allowing the researcher to evolve conclusions pertaining to the learner. The theory does not constitute concern for equality among students as pertains to achievement. Comparing students, studies have shown definitive strength in multimedia learning in an educational setting (Mayer & Anderson, 1991, 1992; Mayer, 1989; Mayer & Sims, 1994). Similarly, the theoretically grounded investigative manner consistently establishes the continued scholarly consideration.

The theory does not avoid the critique that questions whether media have any influence on education. Research, however claims that no credible evidence shows learning benefits from any media that cannot be explained by other non-media factors (Clark, 2001; Clark & Salomon, 1986; Mielke, 1968; Salomon, 1984; Schramm, 1977).

Clark (1994) in his article titled "Media Will Never Influence Learning" questioned the "unique contributions of media attributes" and stated, "[A] number of very different media attributes served the same or similar cognitive" (p. 1). The point of that statement was to establish that no single media attribute is the unique cognitive effect for learning. This would support his point that media is not the defining variable that is instrumental in the considered learning.

Clark (1994) continued with claims that media also are "not directly responsible for motivating learning" (p. 2). He agreed with Salomon (1984), who drew on then new cognitive theories that "attribute motivation to learners' beliefs and expectations about their reactions to external events—not to external events alone" (p. 2). Clark's overarching point remained, which pushed the notion of multimedia being a bystander in educational processes as alternate variable influence learning.

In addition, Clark and Feldon (2005) stated, "[T]he impressive breadth of multimedia formats for instruction and learning may invite a confounding of the specific factors that influence (or fail to influence) learning and motivation for different people and different tasks" (p. 98). They identify that even critics of this conclusion about multimedia—for example, Robert Kozma (1994)—have acknowledged that "no evidence exists to support the argument that media has influenced learning in past research" (p. 98).

Clark and Mayer (2011) further established the core principles of multimedia learning and suggested that course designers should eliminate all embellishments to the learning "added for motivation." The consensus is that these elements are a distraction from learning while simultaneously seducing them by "priming inappropriate existing knowledge" (p. 142). In turn, the deduction is established that multimedia can benefit learning if the core learning seems "boring" (p. 137).

Overarching concerns about multimedia revolve around authors claiming lack of evidence to support definitive gains from multimedia. At the same time, at a minimum, acknowledgment exists to support that an entertainment factor provides initial gains in potentially unexciting learning environments.

EXEMPLARS

Mayer and Anderson (1991, 1992) conducted a study that supported the *multiple representation* principle. Students who were played a narration and simultaneously viewed a corresponding animation explaining how a bicycle tire pump worked rendered twice as many "useful solutions to subsequent problem-solving transfer questions" as students who were offered only the narration (p. 2).

In addition, Mayer (1989) supported the same principle with a study establishing that students who read a text possessing illustrations near the corresponding words rendered "about 65 percent more useful solutions on a subsequent problem-solving transfer test" when compared to students who were offered only text. Mayer (1997) refers to this as the *multimedia effect*. The same studies by Mayer and Anderson (1991, 1992) supported the *contiguity* and *split-attention* principles. The same student group when viewing a corresponding animation to the audio narration rendered 50 percent more useful solutions to subsequent problem-solving transfer questions than those who viewed the animation either before or after the narration. In addition, these students when viewing an animation illustrating the evolution of lightning while simultaneously listening to a corresponding narration rendered 50 percent more useful solutions on a subsequent problem-solving transfer test than students who viewed an identical animation with the narration depicted verbatim on-screen as text.

Mayer and Sims (1994) established the *supporting individual differences* principle, in which students who scored higher on spatial ability tests showed greater multimedia effects than their lower scoring spatial counterparts. Ruth Schwartz (2010) found that "multimedia environments afford learners the opportunity not just to act, but to interact and it is these interactions that provide such rich opportunities for learning" (p. 2).

When examining interactivity in a multimedia environment, Schwartz (2010) discovered an "advantage of looking over listening," demonstrating the multimedia principle (p. 103). When examining whether spatial ability was significant for individual learning, Schwartz (2010) found no statistically significant effects. Nevertheless, "individuals with higher spatial ability did somewhat better" on immediate testing; however, the lower spatial learners had "an advantage in all conditions" on delayed testing (Schwartz, 2010, pp. 108–109).

In a study addressing cognitive load in a multimedia environment applying to age, DaCosta (2008) states, "[M]ultimedia learning environments can impose too high a demand on working memory" (p. iii). DaCosta's study examined the applicability of the modality effect to middle-aged learners in the context of multimedia learning. The experimental group received animation with concurrent narration multimedia learning treatment whereas the comparison group received the same treatment but with concurrent text. The study tested recall on the formation of lightning, much like a study by Mayer and Moreno (1998).

DaCosta's (2008) findings were in disagreement with the Mayer and Moreno (1998) study, which consistently predicted dual-processing theory. Later, the Moreno and Mayer (1999) study revealed a modality effect and found that "mixed-modality presentations are superior to the most integrated text and visual presentations" (p. 366). This was consistent with Paivio's (1986) theory that when learners concurrently maintain words in auditory working memory and pictures in visual working memory, they are offered increased opportunity to focus attention resources to frame connections. DaCosta (2008) acknowledged reasoning for variance in findings included ages, sample size, and the nature of observation.

CONCLUSION

The historical and theoretical evolution of multimedia learning theory merges a number of theories concerned with cognition and learning. Mayer's multimedia learning theory (Clark & Mayer, 2011; Mayer, 1989, 1996, 1997, 2005, 2006; Mayer & Anderson, 1991, 1992; Mayer, Bove, Bryman, Mars, & Tapangco, 1996; Mayer & Moreno, 1998, 2003; Mayer & Sims, 1994) offers a well-grounded theoretical lens for multimedia instructional design, creation of multimedia learning context and environments, and understanding cognition and learning as multimedia information is created and aligned with the diverse needs of learners.

Multimedia learning theory emphasizes the importance of a learner-centered approach to instruction; the learner is most important in teaching and learning. As media and digital technologies have evolved in society, and the integration of media and technologies advances in educational settings, multimedia learning theory presents a lens for advancing teaching and learning in school and university classrooms.

REFERENCES

Asimov, I. (1986). Forward. In J. Hooper & D. Teresi, *The three-pound universe*. New York, NY: Macmillan.

Ayres, P., & Sweller, J. (2005). The split-attention principle in multimedia learning. In R. E. Mayer (Author), *The Cambridge handbook of multimedia learning* (pp. 135–146). Cambridge, UK: Cambridge University Press.

Baddeley, A. D. (1986). *Working memory*. Oxford, UK: Clarendon Press.

Baddeley, A. D. (1992). Working memory. *Science, 255*(5044), 556–559.
Baddeley, A. D. (1999). *Essentials of human memory.* Hove, England: Psychology Press.
Bergeron, L. (2005). Rite of passage for first-year medical school students: Meeting their cadavers. Retrieved from http://news.stanford.edu/news/2005/september14/med-anatomy-091405.html.
Betrancourt, M. (2005). The animation and interactivity principles in multimedia learning. In R. E. Mayer (Author), *The Cambridge handbook of multimedia learning* (pp. 287–296). Cambridge, UK: Cambridge University Press.
Brooks, D. W. (1997). *Web-teaching: A guide to designing interactive teaching for the World Wide Web.* New York, NY: Plenum Press.
Chandler, P., & Sweller, J. (1991). Cognitive load theory and the format of instruction. *Ethics & Behavior, 8*(4), 293–332.
Clark, J. M., & Paivio, A. (1991). Dual coding theory and education. *Educational Psychology Review, 3*(3), 149–210.
Clark, R. C., & Mayer, R. E. (2011). *E-learning and the science of instruction: Proven guidelines for consumers and designers of multimedia learning.* San Francisco, CA: Pfeiffer.
Clark, R. E. (1994). Media will never influence learning. *Educational Technology Research and Development, 42*(2), 21–29.
Clark, R. E. (2001). *Learning from media.* Greenwich, CT: Information Age Publishing.
Clark, R. E., & Feldon, D. F. (2005). Five common but questionable principles of multimedia learning. In R. E. Mayer (Ed.), *The Cambridge handbook of multimedia learning* (pp. 97–115). Cambridge, UK: Cambridge University Press.
Clark, R. E., & Salomon, G. (1986). Media in teaching. In M. C. Wittrock (Ed.), *Handbook of research on teaching* (pp. 464–478). New York, NY: Macmillan.
DaCosta, B. (2008). *The effect of cognitive aging on multimedia learning* (doctoral dissertation). Available from Proquest Dissertations and Theses database. (UMI No. 3319235).
de Jong, T. (2005). The guided discovery principle in multimedia learning. In R. E. Mayer (Ed.), *The Cambridge handbook of multimedia learning* (pp. 215–228). Cambridge, UK: Cambridge University Press.
Fletcher, J. D., & Tobias, S. (2005). The multimedia principle. In R. E. Mayer (Ed.), *The Cambridge handbook of multimedia learning* (pp. 117–133). Cambridge, UK: Cambridge University Press.
Greenlaw, R., & Hepp, E. (1999). *In-line/on-line: Fundamentals of the internet and World Wide Web.* Boston, MA: McGraw-Hill.
Gyimesi, K. (2009, November). *2010 media industry fact sheet* (Rep.). Retrieved from https://www.scribd.com/document/24812446/Nielsen-Fact-Sheet-2010.
Hooper, J., & Teresi, D. (1986). *The three-pound universe.* New York, NY: Macmillan.
Hyde, T. S., & Jenkins, J. J. (1973). Recall for words as a function of semantic, graphic, and syntactic orienting tasks. *Journal of Verbal Learning and Verbal Behavior, 12*(5), pp. 471–480.

Inkpen, K. (1997). Three important research agendas for educational multimedia: Learning, children, and gender. *AACE World Conference on Educational Multimedia and Hypermedia, 97*, 521–526.

Internet World Stats. (2011). Internet growth statistics. Retrieved from https://www.internetworldstats.com/emarketing.htm.

Isger, S. (2011, May 30). FAU medical school to use hands-on approach. *Palm Beach Post*. Retrieved from http://www.palmbeachpost.com.

Jonassen, D. H., Lee, C. B., Yang, C., & Laffey, J. (2005). The collaboration principle in multimedia learning. In R. E. Mayer (Ed.), *The Cambridge handbook of multimedia learning* (pp. 247–270). Cambridge, UK: Cambridge University Press.

Kalyuga, S. (2005). Prior knowledge principle in multimedia learning. In R. E. Mayer (Ed.), *The Cambridge handbook of multimedia learning* (pp. 325–337). Cambridge, UK: Cambridge University Press.

Kozma, R. B. (1994). Will media influence learning? Reframing the debate. *Educational Technology Research and Development, 42*(2), 7–19.

Larkin, M. (2006). Rx for survival: A global health challenge. *The Lancet Infectious Diseases, 6*(1), 18–19.

Lockee, B. B., Burton, J. K., & Cross, L. H. (1999). No comparison: Distance education finds a new use for 'no significant difference.' *Educational Technology Research and Development, 47*(3), 33–42.

Low, R., & Sweller, J. (2005). The modality principle in multimedia learning. In R. E. Mayer (Ed.), *The Cambridge handbook of multimedia learning* (pp. 147–158). Cambridge, UK: Cambridge University Press.

Mayer, R. E. (1989). Systematic thinking fostered by illustrations in scientific text. *Journal of Educational Psychology, 81*(2), 240–246.

Mayer, R. E. (1996). Learning strategies for making sense out of expository text: The SOI model for guiding three cognitive processes in knowledge construction. *Educational Psychology Review, 8*(4), 357–371.

Mayer, R. E. (1997). Multimedia learning: Are we asking the right questions? *Educational Psychologist, 32*(1), 1–19.

Mayer, R. E. (2005). Introduction to *multimedia learning*. In R. E. Mayer (Ed.), The Cambridge handbook of multimedia learning (pp. 1–18). Cambridge, UK: Cambridge University Press.

Mayer, R. E. (2006). Ten research-based principles of multimedia learning. In H. F. O'Neil & R. S. Perez (Authors), *Web-based learning: Theory, research, and practice* (pp. 371–390). Mahwah, NJ: Lawrence Erlbaum Associates.

Mayer, R. E., & Anderson, R. B. (1991). Animations need narrations: An experimental test of a dual-coding hypothesis. *Journal of Educational Psychology, 83*(4), 484–490.

Mayer, R. E., & Anderson, R. B. (1992). The instructive animation: Helping students build connections between words and pictures in multimedia learning. *Journal of Educational Psychology, 84*(4), 444–452.

Mayer, R. E., Bove, W., Bryman, A., Mars, R., & Tapangco, L. (1996). When less is more: Meaningful learning from visual and verbal summaries of science textbook lessons. *Journal of Educational Psychology, 88*(1), 64–73.

Mayer, R. E., & Moreno, R. (1998). A split-attention effect in multimedia learning: Evidence for dual processing systems in working memory. *Journal of Educational Psychology, 90*(2), 312–320.

Mayer, R. E., & Moreno, R. (2003). Nine ways to reduce cognitive load in multimedia learning. *Educational Psychologist, 38*(1), 43–52.

Mayer, R. E., & Sims, V. K. (1994). For whom is a picture worth a thousand words? Extensions of a dual-coding theory of multimedia learning. *Journal of Educational Psychology, 86*(3), 389–401.

Mielke, K. W. (1968). Questioning the questions of ETV research. *Educational Broadcasting, 2*, 6–15.

Miniwatts Marketing Group. (2011). *Internet world stats: Usage and population statistics.* Retrieved from http://www.internetworldstats.com/.

Moreno, R., & Mayer, R. E. (1999). Cognitive principles of multimedia learning: The role of modality and contiguity. *Journal of Educational Psychology, 91*(2), 358–368.

National Center for Education Statistics (NCES). (2005, May). Retrieved from http://nces.ed.gov/programs/digest/d10/tables/dt10_015.asp.

National Center for Education Statistics (NCES). (2009, December). Retrieved from http://nces.ed.gov/.

National Center for Education Statistics (NCES). (2010, August). Retrieved from http://nces.ed.gov/programs/digest/d10/tables/dt10_108.asp.

Paas, F., Van Gerven, P. W., & Tabbers, H. K. (2005). The cognitive aging principle in multimedia learning. In R. E. Mayer (Ed.), *The Cambridge handbook of multimedia learning* (pp. 339–351). Cambridge, UK: Cambridge University Press.

Paivio, A. (1963). Learning of adjective-noun paired associates as a function of adjective-noun word. *Canadian Journal of Psychology, 17*, 370–379.

Paivio, A. (1965). Abstractness, imagery, and meaningfulness in paired-associate learning. *Journal of Verbal Learning and Verbal Behavior, 4*(1), 32–38.

Paivio, A. (1986). *Mental representations: A dual coding approach.* New York, NY: Oxford University Press.

Paivio, A. (1991). Dual coding theory: Retrospect and current status. *Canadian Journal of Psychology Revue Canadienne De Psychologie, 45*(3), 255–287.

Passig, D., & Levin, H. (1999). Gender interest differences with multimedia learning interfaces among preschoolers. *Computers in Human Behavior, 15*(2), 173–183.

Renkl, A. (2005). The worked-out examples principle in multimedia learning. In R. E. Mayer (Ed.), *The Cambridge handbook of multimedia learning* (pp. 229–245). Cambridge, UK: Cambridge University Press.

Rouet, J., & Potelle, H. (2005). Navigational principles in multimedia learning. In R. E. Mayer (Ed.), *The Cambridge handbook of multimedia learning* (pp. 297–312). Cambridge, UK: Cambridge University Press.

Roy, M., & Chi, M. T. (2005). The self-explanation principle in multimedia learning. In R. E. Mayer (Ed.), *The Cambridge handbook of multimedia learning* (pp. 271–286). Cambridge, UK: Cambridge University Press.

Salomon, G. (1984). Television is "easy" and print is "tough": The differential investment of mental effort in learning as a function of perceptions and attributions. *Journal of Educational Psychology, 76*(4), 647–658.

Schramm, W. (1977). *Big media, little media: Tools and technologies for instruction.* Beverly Hills, CA: Sage Publications.

Schwartz, J. E., & Beichner, R. J. (1999). *Essentials of educational technology.* Boston, MA: Allyn & Bacon.

Schwartz, R. N. (2010). *Considering the activity in interactivity: A multimodal perspective* (doctoral dissertation). Available from ProQuest Dissertations and Theses database. (UMI No. 3404551).

Shapiro, A. M. (2005). The site map principle in multimedia learning. In R. E. Mayer (Ed.), *The Cambridge handbook of multimedia learning* (pp. 313–324). Cambridge, UK: Cambridge University Press.

Smith, C. (2011, April 13). Egypt's Facebook revolution: Wael ghonim thanks the social network. *Huffington Post.* Retrieved from http://www.huffingtonpost.com/.

Sweller, J. (1988). Cognitive load during problem solving: Effects on learning. *Cognitive Science, 12*(2), 257–285.

Sweller, J. (1999). *Instructional design in technical areas.* Camberwell, Vic: ACER Press.

Sweller, J. (2005). The redundancy principle in multimedia learning. In R. E. Mayer (Ed.), *The Cambridge handbook of multimedia learning* (pp. 159–167). Cambridge, UK: Cambridge University Press.

Tobias, S. (1989). Another look at research on the adaptation of instruction to students characteristics. *Educational Psychologist, 24*(3), 213–227.

United States Census Bureau. (2013). Retrieved from https://www.census.gov/prod/2013pubs/p20-569.pdf.

Willingham, D. T. (2009). *Why don't students like school? A cognitive scientist answers questions about how the mind works and what it means for the classroom.* San Francisco, CA: Jossey-Bass.

Yates, F. A. (1966). *The art of memory.* Chicago, IL: University of Chicago Press.

Chapter 3

Multimedia Learning Theory and Its Implications for Teaching and Learning

Patrick M. Jenlink

INTRODUCTION

The present-day spectrum of multimedia and digital technologies and implications for these technologies on learning environments in educational settings draw attention to new and emerging considerations for teaching and learning (Jones & Shao, 2011). Equally important, the implications for multimedia learning theory as it relates to the teacher and learner focus attention on the design of multimedia innovation in instruction and curriculum. Specifically, multimedia learning theory presents significant implications for how we teach, what we teach, and the interface between multimedia learning theory, media and digital technologies, instructional design, and the cognitive needs of the learner (Clark, 2009; Mayer, 2009).

When considering multiple forms of media integrated into instructional messages as visual and auditory/verbal messaging (Mayer, 2008a, 2009) of instructional content that aligns with different cognitive learning needs of the learner, acknowledge that each student learns differently and has different needs. Multimedia learning theory enables the teacher as instructional designer to integrate media-based messaging that presents content that the learner can then align with his preference for acquiring and integrating information into the existing cognitive schemas[1] or memory.

Therefore, multimedia learning theory applied to instructional design enables students to learn about abstract principles through text (auditory/verbal) and see the application of those principles through an animation or a video example (visual) (Mayer 2008a, 2008b).[2] This presents the opportunity for deeper levels of understanding, particularly if the multimedia instructional messaging aligns with potential for learner interaction, which is predicated on understanding cognition.

An important implication of multimedia learning theory is related to changing the nature of teaching and learning from a teacher-centered approach to a learner-centered approach to fostering learning in the classroom. The implication of multimedia learning theory is that it enables teachers/instructors to integrate text, graphics, animation, and other media into a multimedia instructional message or presentation, including both visual and auditory/verbal content for an enriched learning experience (de Sousa, Richter, & Nel, 2017; Jarosievitz, 2009, 2011).

Research supports multimedia learning effectiveness in instructional design and teaching in biology (Satyaprakasha & Sudhanshu, 2014), early childhood education (Shilpa & Sunita, 2013), teaching English (Shyamlee & Phil, 2012; Zhen, 2016), foreign language acquisition (Almekhlafi, 2006; Amine, Benachaiba, & Guemide, 2012; Farias, Obilinovic, & Orrego, 2007; Zhang & Zhao, 2013), mathematics (Malik, 2011; Milovanovic, Obradovic, & Mulajic, 2013; Nusir, Alsmadi, Al-Kabi, & Sharadgah, 2012), science (Ercan, 2014; Eskandari & Ebrahimi, 2013; Kapri, 2017; Schrader, 2016), social studies (de Sousa, Richter, & Nel, 2017), students with learning disabilities (Greer, Crutchfield, & Woods, 2013), medical practices (Chang & Hsu, 2010; Genuchten, Hooijdonk, Schuler, & Scheiter, 2014; Yu-ling & Yu-Hsiu, 2014), political science (Udim & Etim, 2016), professional military education (Bradbeer & Porter, 2017), and technical education (Stebila, 2011). The scope of these studies in relation to disciplines and content area indicate the emerging importance of multimedia learning.

This chapter explores the implications of multimedia learning theory for teaching and learning, with a focus on three areas: instruction, cognition, and the learner. Although the implications apply to additional areas, these three are primary. The position taken in this chapter is that teaching in the multimedia learning environment is predicated on the interface between instruction, cognition, and the needs of the learner.

MULTIMEDIA LEARNING AND INSTRUCTION

Sweller (2005) explains that "good instructional design is driven by our knowledge of human cognitive structures and the manner in which those structures are organized" (p. 20). As the cognitive structures are used to learn, think, and solve problems, they form a cognitive architecture. The integration of multimedia learning theory in instructional design and instructional messaging using both visual and audio/verbal messages leads to developing the learner's cognitive architecture.

Multimedia learning theory focuses attention on both visual and auditory/verbal content in instructional design and messaging (Mayer, 2008a, 2009) while cognitive theory focuses attention on relationships between long-term and working memory (Sweller, 2005). Interface between the two theories lies in how the messaging of content is transformed into knowledge. As Sweller has explained, "[T]he nature of those relations provides the center-piece of human cognitive functioning and is critical to any theory of instructional design" (p. 24).

Instructional Design and Content Delivery

Content delivery is a major component of instruction. The purpose of multimedia instruction is the delivery of different forms of content to enable knowledge conveyance from instructor to student. Multimedia instructional design and messaging effectiveness depend upon the design and interaction between instructor and student.[3]

Equally important, the multimedia delivery medium (mixed visual and audio/verbal) aligned with the differentiation in learning modalities and cognitive needs of the learner requires a level of interactivity (Mayer, 2008a, 2008b). The learning environment and the nature of the content to be delivered in concert with interactive learning enable the content from the instructional message to enter the learner's working memory and subsequently long-term memory and be integrated into the learner's cognitive architecture.

Modes of instruction delivery depend on instructional design and the forms of media integrated in the design of the instructional message. For instance, smart classrooms that are equipped with state-of-the-art multimedia technology give instructors a wide range of options to suit nearly every instruction style and align with learner modalities of learning. The types of technologies (i.e., media or digital, interactive, or social media) incorporated in multimedia instructional design are left to instructors to decide. The nature of interactivity and discovery in multimedia learning and instructional design affords opportunity to move beyond more traditional and passive learning (Mayer & Sims, 1994; Mayer, 2000).

Interactive versus Noninteractive Learning

Multimedia instruction is concerned with interactive learning, and the design of instructional messages for multimedia learning differentiates between interactive and noninteractive learning (Moreno & Mayer, 2007).[4] Designing multimedia instruction focuses on a "continuum of interactivity in learning environments ranging from highly interactive—which allow[s] for strong communication between the learner and the instructional system, to non-interactive—which do[es] not allow for communication between the learner and the instructional system" (Moreno & Mayer, 2007, p. 311).

When designing multimedia instruction, instructional design issues using both extremes of the interactivity continuum warrant consideration.[5] Designing multimedia instructional messaging requires that the type of media as well as the learning modalities be considered in relation to interactive learning. Multimedia instructional messages, especially those that combine words (auditory/verbal) and pictorial (visual) representations of knowledge according to the multimedia principle (Mayer, 2005a), can enhance student understanding by the addition of nonverbal knowledge representations to verbal explanations.[6]

Mixed Modalities of Instructional Design

According to the modality principle of instructional design (Low & Sweller, 2005; Mayer, 2005c; Moreno 2006; Moreno & Mayer, 2007), the most effective learning environments are those whose instructional design combines verbal and nonverbal representations of the knowledge using mixed-modality presentations. Moreno and Mayer (2007) explain: "[B]ecause human cognitive architecture includes independent, limited capacity, processing channels, the presentation of verbal and non-verbal materials in the visual modality alone is more likely to overload learners' cognitive capacity during learning" (p. 310). Moreno and Mayer (2007) explain: "[B]ecause human cognitive architecture includes independent, limited capacity, processing channels, the presentation of verbal and non-verbal materials in the visual modality alone is more likely to overload learners' cognitive capacity during learning" (p. 310), in contrast to "the presentation of verbal materials in the auditory modality and non-verbal materials in the visual modality" (p. 310).

MULTIMEDIA LEARNING AND COGNITION

The cognitive theory of multimedia learning, one of several cognitivist learning theories, originally was introduced by American psychology professor Richard Mayer in the 1990s (Mayer, 1997, 1999a, 1999b; Mayer & Anderson, 1991, 1992). It is a sub-theory of John Sweller's cognitive load theory (Sweller, 1988, 1994, 1999, 2003). Mayer's theory of cognitive multimedia learning, as applied specifically to multimedia learning and instructional design, has many similarities to Sweller's cognitive load theory.

Cognitive Load Theory

A basic assumption of Mayer's theory is that the human working memory has two subcomponents that work in parallel (visual and auditory/verbal) and that learning can be more successful if both of these channels are used for information processing at the same time. Cognitive load theory describes how the architecture of cognition has specific implications for the design of multimedia learning instruction (Sweller, 2003). According to Sweller (2005), "[T]here are three categories of cognitive load discussed by the theory: extraneous, intrinsic, and germane cognitive load" (p. 26).

In relation to multimedia instructional design, extraneous cognitive load results when "inappropriate instructional designs that [sic] ignore working memory limits and fail to focus working memory resources on schema construction and automation" (p. 26). Extraneous cognitive load is created by unnecessary information that usurps cognitive capacity that could otherwise be used for handling germane and intrinsic cognitive load; extraneous load is often a result of poor instructional design (de Jong, 2010).

When considering the natural complexity of the information presented for processing, "intrinsic cognitive load . . . is determined by the levels of elements interactivity" (Sweller, 2005, p. 27) in the multimedia learning experience. Intrinsic cognitive load is the inherent level of difficulty associated with instructional materials, directly tied to information or content. Generally, content that is simple with few interacting elements has a lower intrinsic cognitive load. Content that is high in interactivity requires more cognitive resources to process and, therefore, has higher intrinsic cognitive load.

Germane cognitive load, as Sweller explains, is "effective cognitive load . . . caused by effortful learning resulting in schema construction and automation" (Sweller, 2005, p. 27). Germane cognitive load is referred to as good cognitive load placed on the working memory during schema construction and knowledge building. Cognitive load theory as the parent theory for cognitive multimedia learning theory suggests that multimedia instruction should be designed in a way that recognizes working memory channels and load limitations so that learners can thoroughly process new content (de Jong, 2010; Kirschner, 2002; Sweller, Van Merriënboer, & Paas, 1998).

Cognitive Multimedia Theory Applications

Cognitive multimedia theory has broad applications in the design of multimedia instructional messaging/presentation, providing a general framework and conceptual map for multimedia instructional designers to minimize and control the conditions that create unwanted cognitive load in learning (de Jong, 2010). Research has revealed that deeper learning is achieved when the following multimedia combinations are used: text and picture explanations rather than verbal explanations; exclusion of irrelevant words, sounds, and video; avoidance of complex verbal and pictorial representations with no guidance for low prior-knowledge learners; and words presented in a personalized, conversational style (Mayer, 2005b, 2005c; Mayer & Moreno, 2003; Moreno & Mayer, 2007).

MULTIMEDIA LEARNING AND THE LEARNER

When considering multimedia learning and the learner, the key is to leverage multimedia and digital technologies to enhance learner interaction with the course content. Learning, as related to multimedia instruction, is defined as "an alteration in long-term memory. If nothing has altered in long-term memory nothing has been learned. Accordingly, appropriate alterations to long-term memory should be the primary aim of instruction" (Sweller, 2005, p. 20).

Multimedia learning, as a media and digital technology-based learning experience, enables the learner to engage with instructional content and solve problems by means of self-exploration, collaboration, and active participation. Simulations, models, and media-rich study materials (still and animated graphics, video and audio) integrated in a structured manner can facilitate the learning of new knowledge. Multimedia learning encourages and enhances peer learning, individual creativity, and innovation (Malik & Agarwal, 2012).

Multimedia and the Learner

As the learner experiences the multimedia instructional message or presentation with both visual and auditory/verbal content, the learner must select relevant aspects of the incoming messages (content) for processing, which is the *dual channel processes*. The second set of processes for the learner is to build a coherent mental representation of the auditory/verbal material (i.e., form a verbal model) and a coherent mental representation of the visual material (i.e., form a pictorial model). These processes are called *organizing*. A third process is to build connections between the verbal and pictorial models and with prior knowledge. These processes are called *integrating*.

The processes of selecting, organizing, and integrating generally do not occur in a rigid linear order, but rather in an iterative fashion. Once a learning outcome has been constructed, it is stored in long-term memory for future use. Meaningful learning depends on all three of these processes occurring for the visual and auditory/verbal representations. According to Mayer (2005b, 2005c), learners engage in active learning (such as the processes of selecting, organizing, and integrating) even when the presentation media do not allow hands-on activity (such as printed text and illustrations, or animation and narration).

Multimedia learning, in addition to instructional messages or presentations, is concerned with collaborative and participatory learning experiences. Collaborative represents a socially mediated activity whereas participatory represents direct involvement in the creation of the multimedia message or presentation of content.

Collaborative Multimedia Learning

Multimedia and digital technologies for learning represent multimedia instructional design options that can transform cognition and learning. Collaborative learning constitutes a socially mediated activity in which the knowledge is built in a combined, located, and distributed way from the dynamic interaction established between the learners, the sociocultural environment in which the activity is developed, and the cultural instruments used for such activity (Acuña & López-Aymes, 2016).

The selection of media and digital technologies integrated into designing instructional messages and group activity requires that the instructional design accommodate the learners' modalities of learning, considering how to create activities that engage the learners to socially construct knowledge through problem solving.[7] Multimedia learning in this sense requires collaborative processes in order to facilitate the emergence of productive interaction. Dawson (2008) explains that interactivity and use of multiple media and digital technologies in learning enhance the students' learning process and provide a beneficial alternative to passive traditional learning.

Collaborative multimedia learning instructional design supports the "activation of highly elaborated exchanges about the contents presented in the multimedia, bringing the comprehension through the discussion in which different ideas and points of view are revealed" (p. 85) and the "explicitness of abilities ... kept implicit in individual tasks, especially the regulatory abilities related with the planning, monitoring, and the evaluation of the process that are required to put into play to achieve a shared deep comprehension of these multimedia contents" (Acuña & López-Aymes, 2016, p. 85).

Participatory Multimedia Learning

One of the challenges of designing multimedia learning instruction is engaging students in participatory learning (Kiili, 2005). Participatory multimedia learning requires learning with instructional systems that enable learners to produce part of the learning texts (visual and auditory/verbal instructional content). The focus of participatory multimedia learning is to represent the human information processing system more exhaustively than its predecessor, the cognitive theory of multimedia learning (Mayer, 2005a, 2005b), and to support the transformation of cognitive resources into the germane cognitive load needed for knowledge construction (Sweller, 2005).

Multimedia integration in the teaching and learning environment has made it possible for learners to become involved in their work and create multimedia applications as part of their multimedia instructional activity. Multimedia, in this way, enables the learner to become an active participant in the multimedia learning, making use of the knowledge presented by the teacher/instructor, and represent learner needs in a more meaningful way, using different media elements.

Interactive and Discovery Multimedia Learning

Interactive multimedia offers an alternative medium of instruction to the more traditional teacher-centered learning experience (Allen, 2003). Interactivity and discovery in multimedia learning offer an alternative to passive learning. Rather than be bounded by the pace of the teacher, learners are individually paced according to their own ability. One way that multimedia can give low-ability students, or students with disabilities, extensive learning time before moving forward is to design instruction that accommodates the learner's needs and provides multimedia interface that allows the learner to move at his own pace.

Alternatively, high-ability students can branch out to random sequencing through the multimedia instructional messaging and not be confined by linearity or a much slower pace. This aspect of multimedia learning supports a learner-centered strategy whereby learners take responsibility in their own learning process. In the learner-centered mode, the learner takes an active part in her learning process and becomes an autonomous learner actively engaged in constructing new meaning within the context of her current knowledge, experiences, and social environments. Interactivity is a critical component of teaching and learning. The cognitive activity of multimedia learning is designed to be encouraging and directive.

CONCLUSIONS

Ultimately, multimedia learning theory guides the structure of multimedia content and instruction, the relationship between teaching and learning, to take full advantage of how the brain processes incoming visual and auditory information for the purpose of creating quality multimedia instructional materials for learners.

Our innate beliefs as educators about such things as how we think people learn are often unstated, but they serve as the "operating system" upon which we base our instructional decisions in the classroom. Change in the learning environment of the classroom, away from teacher-centered to learning-centered, requires a change in the operating system that guides our decisions. The implications of multimedia learning theory for transforming teaching and learning in classrooms and educational settings are far-reaching.

Multimedia learning theory enables us to connect to the new generation of learners entering the classroom, learners who already are practiced in the use of media and digital technologies. The realization in this understanding is that integrating multimedia learning theory into our instructional design, changing our "operating system" of how we understand cognition and learning, enables us to transform the classroom and ourselves as educators.

NOTES

1. Sweller (2005) explains that schemas are cognitive constructs that allow multiple elements of information to be categorized as a single element and entered into long-term memory. In relation to learning, "all skilled performance in complex domains requires the acquisition of countless numbers of schemas held in long-term memory" (p. 21). Sweller further explains, "[W]hen brought into working memory from long-term memory, a schema allows us to treat multiple elements of information as a single element classified according to the way in which it will be used" (p. 29).

2. Mayer (2005a, 2005b, 2005c) explains that the auditory/verbal and visual are the basis for a dual channel assumption, which states that humans possess separate information processing systems for visual and verbal representations. For example, animations are processed in the visual/pictorial channel and spoken words (i.e., narrations) are processed in the auditory/verbal channel.

3. Integrated instruction represents multiple sources of information (visual and auditory/verbal) that are physically integrated through instructional design "so that working memory resources do not need to be used for mental integration" (Sweller, 2005, p. 29).

4. Mayer (2004) explains that interactivity and the need for learners to make inferences is often not as effective as direct instruction in promoting meaningful learning. Therefore, it is especially important to determine the conditions under which interactivity promotes knowledge construction as a consideration for the design of multimedia instructional messaging.

5. Moreno and Mayer (2007) explain that "a non-interactive multimodal learning environment is a multimedia explanation: a linear presentation including verbal and visual representations of the scientific system to-be-learned" (p. 312).

6. Moreno and Mayer (2007) explain that the nonverbal mode is the pictorial mode, which includes static graphics (such as photos, illustrations, graphs, drawings, and maps) and dynamic graphics (such as video and animation).

7. A collaborative multimedia learning activity requires instructional scaffolding in which social interaction is enriched and allows exchanges, which drives the embracement of roles played in the group activity, and new functions or the restructuring of the existent ones are internalized.

REFERENCES

Acuña, S. R., & López-Aymes, G. (2016). Collaborative multimedia learning: Influence of a social regulatory support on learning performance and on collaboration. *Journal of Curriculum and Teaching, 5*(2), 83–94.

Alexander, R. J. (Ed.). (2010). *Children, their world, their education: Final report and recommendations of the Cambridge Primary Review*. London, England: Routledge.

Allen, M. W. (2003). *Guide to e-learning: Building interactive, fun and effective learning programs for any company*. Hoboken, NJ: John Wiley & Sons.

Almekhlafi, A. G. (2006). The effect of Computer Assisted Language Learning (CALL) on United Arab Emirates English as a Foreign Language (EFL) school students' achievement and attitude. *Journal of Interactive Learning Research, 17*(2), 121–142.

Amine, B. M., Benachaiba, C., & Guemide, B. (2012). Using multimedia to motivate students in EFL classrooms: A case study of English master's students at Jikel University, Algeria. *Malaysian Journal of Distance Education, 14*(2), 63–81.

Bradbeer, T. G., & Porter, S. A. (2017). Enhancing learning using multimedia in professional military education. *Journal of Military Learning, 1*(2), 56–68.

Chang, M., & Hsu, L. (2010). Multimedia instruction: Its efficacy in nurse electrocardiography learning [Chinese]. *Journal of Nursing, 57*(4), 50–58.

Clark, R. E. (2009). Translating research into new instructional technologies for higher education: The active ingredient process. *Journal of Computing in Higher Education, 21*, 4–18.

Dawson, C. (2008). Web modules: Integrating curricula and technology standards. *AACE Journal, 16*(1), 3–20. Retrieved from https://digitalscholarship.tsu.edu/sbaj/vol16/iss1/2.

de Jong, T. (2010). Cognitive load theory, educational research, and instructional design: Some food for thought. *Instructional Science, 28*, 105–134.

Desai, M. S., & Ojode, L. (2017). Implications of social media use on instruction and student learning: An exploratory study. *Southwestern Business Administration Journal, 16*(1).

de Sousa, L., Richter, B., & Nel, C. (2017). The effect of multimedia use on the teaching and learning of social studies at tertiary level: A case study. *Yesterday & Today, 17*, 1–22. doi:http://dx.doi.org/10.17159/2223-0386/2017/n17a1.

Ercan, O. (2014). The effects of multimedia learning material on students' academic achievement and attitudes towards science courses. *Journal of Baltic Science Education, 13*(5), 608–621.

Eskandari, Z., & Ebrahimi, N. A. (2013). Effects of computure and multimedia software on Iranian high school students' learning and perceptions of chemistry classroom environments. *International Jouranl of Technology in Teaching and Learning, 9*(2), 159–172.

Farias, M., Obilinovic, K., & Orrego, R. (2007). Implications of multimedia learning models on foreign language teaching and learning. *Columbian Applied Linguistics Journal, 9*, 174–199.

Genuchten, E., Hooijdonk, C., Schüler, A., & Scheiter, K. (2014). The role of working memory when "learning how" with multimedia learning material. *Applied Cognitive Psychology, 28*(3), 327–335.

Greer, D. L., Crutchfield, S. A., & Woods, K. L. (2013). Cognitive theory of multimedia learning, Instructional design principles, and students with learning disabilities in computer-based and online learning environments. *Technology in Education, 193*(2), 41–50.

Jarosievitz, B. (2009). ICT use in science education. In A. Vilas, A. Marin, J. Gonzalez, & J. A. Gonzalez (Eds.), *Research, reflections, and innovations in integrating ICT in education* (Vol. 1, pp. 382–386). Badajoz, Spain: FORMATEX.

Jarosievitz, B. (2011). ICT, multimedia used in the national and international educational projects. *Informatika, 38*, 22–26.

Jones, C., & Shao, B. (2011). *The net generation and digital natives: Implications for higher education*. York, UK: Higher Education Academy.

Kapri, U. C. (2017). Impact of multimedia in teaching science. *IJARIE, 3*(4), 2179–2187.

Kiili, K. (2005). Participatory multimedia learning: Engaging learners. *Australasian Journal of Educational Technology, 21*(3), 303–322.

Kirschner, P. A. (2002). Cognitive load theory: Implications of cognitive load theory on the design of learning. *Learning and Instruction, 12*(1), 1–10.

Low, R., & Sweller, J. (2005). The modality principle in multimedia learning. In R. E. Mayer (Ed.), *The Cambridge handbook of multimedia learning* (pp. 147–158). New York, NY: Cambridge University Press.

Malik, I. Z. (2011). *Effects of multimedia-based instructional technology on African American ninth grade students' mastery of algebra concepts*. Retrieved from ProQuest (865037802).

Malik, S. & Agarwal, A. (2012). Use of multimedia as a new educational technology tool—A study. *International Journal of Information and Education Technology, 2*(5), 468–471.

Mayer, R. E. (1997). Multimedia learning: Are we asking the right questions? *Educational Psychologist, 32*, 1–19.

Mayer, R. E. (1999a). Multimedia aids to problem-solving transfer. *International Journal of Educational Research, 31*, 611–623.

Mayer, R. E. (1999b). Research-based principles for the design of instructional messages. *Document Design, 1*, 7–20.

Mayer, R. E. (2000). Multimedia learning: Are we asking the right questions? *Educational Psychologist, 32*(1), 1–19.

Mayer, R. E. (2005a). Cognitive theory of multimedia learning. In R. Mayer (Ed.), *Cambridge handbook of multimedia learning* (pp. 31–48). New York, NY: Cambridge University Press.

Mayer, R. E. (2005b). Principles for managing essential processing multimedia learning: Segmenting, pretraining, and modality principles. In R. E. Mayer (Ed.), *Cambridge handbook of multimedia learning* (pp. 169–182). New York, NY: Cambridge University Press.

Mayer, R. E. (2005c). Principles of multimedia learning based on social cues: Personalization, voice, and image principles. In R. E. Mayer (Ed.), *The Cambridge handbook of multimedia learning* (pp. 201–214). Cambridge, UK: Cambridge University Press.

Mayer, R. E. (2008a). Applying the science of learning: Evidence-based principles for the design of multimedia instruction. *American Psychologist, 63*, 760–769.

Mayer, R. E. (2008b). *Learning and instruction* (2nd ed.). Upper Saddle River, NY: Pearson Merrill Prentice Hall.

Mayer, R. E. (2009). *Multimedia learning* (2nd ed.). New York, NY: Cambridge University Press.

Mayer, R. E., & Anderson, R. B. (1991). Animations need narrations: An experimental test of a dual-coding hypothesis. *Journal of Educational Psychology, 83*, 484–490.

Mayer, R. E., & Anderson, R. B. (1992). The instructive animation: Helping students build connections between words and pictures in multimedia learning. *Journal of Educational Psychology, 84*, 444–452.

Mayer, R. E., & Moreno, R. (2003). Nine ways to reduce cognitive load in multimedia learning. *Educational Psychologist, 38*(1), 43–52.

Mayer, R. E., & Sims, V. K. (1994). For whom is a picture worth a thousand words? Extensions of a dual-coding theory of multimedia learning. *Journal of educational Psychology, 86*(3), 389–401.

Milovanovic, M., Obradovic, J., & Milajic, A. (2013). Application of interactive multimedia tools in teaching mathematics—examples of lessons from geometry. TOJET: The Turkish Online *Journal of Educational Technology, 12*(1), 19–31.

Moreno, R. (2006). Does the modality principle hold for different media? A test of the method affects learning hypothesis. *Journal of Computer Assisted Learning, 22*, 149–158.

Moreno, R., & Mayer, R. (2007). Interactive multimodal learning environments. *Educational Psychology Review, 19*, 309–326. doi:10.1007/s10648-007-9047-2.

Nusir, S., Alsmadi, I., Al-Kabi, M., & Sharadgah, F. (2012). Studying the impact of using multimedia interactive programs at children ability to learn basic math skills. *Acta Didactica Napocensia, 5*(2), 17–32.

Satyaprakasha, C. V., & Sudhanshu. Y. (2014). Effect of multi media teaching on achievement in biology. *International Journal of Education and Psychological Research, 3*(1), 41–45.

Schrader, P. G. (2016). Does multimedia theory apply to all students? The impact of multimedia presentations on science learning. *Journal of Learning and Teaching in Digital Age (JOLTIDA), 1*(1), 32–46.

Shilpa, S., & Sunita, M. (2013). A study about role of multimedia in early childhood education. *International Journal of Humanities and Social Science Invention, 61*(2), 80–85.

Shyamlee, S. D., & Phil, M. (2012). Use of technology in English language teaching and learning: An analysis. *IPEDR, 33*, 150–156.

Stebila, J. (2011). Research and prediction of the application of multimedia teaching aid in teaching technical education on the 2nd level of primary school. *Informatics in Education, 10*(1), 105–122.

Sweller, J. (1988). Cognitive load during problem solving: Effects on learning. *Cognitive Science, 12*, 257–285.

Sweller, J. (1994). Cognitive load theory, learning difficulty, and instructional design. *Learning and Instruction, 4*(4), 295–312.

Sweller, J. (1999). *Instructional design in technical areas*. Camberwell, Australia: ACER Press.

Sweller, J. (2003). Evolution of human cognitive architecture. In B. H. Ross (Ed.), *The psychology of learning and motivation* (Vol. 43, pp. 215–266). New York, NY: Academic Press.

Sweller, J. (2005). Implications of cognitive load theory for multimedia learning. In R. E. Mayer (Ed.), *The Cambridge handbook of multimedia learning* (pp. 19–30). Cambridge, UK: Cambridge University Press.

Sweller, J., Van Merriënboer, J., & Paas, F. (1998). Cognitive architecture and instructional design. *Educational Psychology Review, 10*(3), 251–296.

Udim, D. K., & Etim, E. A. (2016). Use of multimedia in teaching and learning of political science in University of Uyo, Akwa Ibom State, Nigeria. *Research in Pedagogy, 6*(2), 154–170.

Yu-Ling, W., & Yu-Hsiu, K. (2014). The effects of multimedia-assisted instruction on the skin care learning of nurse aides in long-term care facilities. *Nursing, 61*(4), 26–34.

Zhang, S., & Zhao, F. (2013). Application of multimedia technology in situational teaching of foreign language. *Journal of Theoretical and Applied Information Technology, 48*(3), 1612–1618.

Zhen, Z. (2016). The use of multimedia in English teaching. *US-China Foreign Language, 14*(3), 182–189.

Chapter 4

Multimedia Learning and the Next Generation Classroom

Patrick M. Jenlink

INTRODUCTION

The classroom of the past and present, at the public school and university level, is decidedly different, due in large part to the advancement of technologies over the past five decades. The classroom of the 1960s was characterized by blackboards (chalk and talk), textbooks, printed assignments, and pedagogical and epistemological practices and perspectives that were traditional and passed down from one generation of educators to the next. The classroom of today, in contrast, can be characterized by whiteboards, digital technologies, and advances in pedagogical and epistemological practices and perspectives as a result of new theories of learning and the internet and digital landscape.

What the future holds for the classroom in schools and universities is yet to be determined; however, the advances in cognitive architectures for multimedia learning and the opportunities for multimedia learning already have changed our understanding of teaching and learning and the preparation of next-generation educators and students. Multimedia, as Reed (2006) notes, "is increasingly providing richer environments for learning by presenting information in a wide variety of different formats" (p. 87).

The students served by the school and university in classrooms of the past and present are equally different, as will be the students of the future. The generation of students entering the classroom of the 1960s did not experience the internet or digital technologies, as these technological advances were just on the horizon of society at that time.

The generation of students entering the classroom today, however, comes with significant experience in the use of the internet and digital technologies; these students have grown up with smart phones and social media. Clarke

(2012) explains that the advance of digital technologies, "from tablets and e-readers to learning management systems and multimedia digital textbooks, continues to evolve and bring new opportunities for educators" (p. 1). As a next generation of learner enters the classroom, "the widespread adoption of tablets, mobile applications, social networks and digital content has led students to expect more interaction via software and digital content as they learn" (p. 1).

Given the advancement in Web-based and digital technologies and the increasingly user-friendly interfaces, an influx of multimedia has become available in the classroom. This chapter examines how the multimedia learning theory can aid in adapting a classroom to best benefit a range of learners, as well as appropriately discern the affect multimedia have on students.

THE INFLUENCE OF MULTIMEDIA ON LEARNING

Kozma (1994), examining the influence of media on learning, asks, "What are the actual and potential relationships between media and learning? Can we describe and understand those relationships? And can we create a strong and compelling influence of media on learning through improved theories, research, and instructional designs?" (p. 1). The author's questions remain as salient today as when first posited more than two decades ago.

Internet access, Web 2.0, and new digital technologies have changed the nature of education substantially. As Clarke (2012) explains, "[C]lassrooms are no longer learning islands" (p. 2). Classrooms infused with multimedia and guided by multimedia learning can become collaborative learning spaces, augmenting and enhancing learning through multimedia interfaces and enriched multimedia presentations that merge verbal and visual learning modalities (Mayer, Hegarty, Mayer, & Cambel, 2005; Mayer & Massa, 2003).

As a multimedia learning space, the learning architecture of the classroom, connected via "digital content development and learning management systems" (Clarke, 2012, p. 2), enables a new level of multimedia enhanced pedagogical practice that acknowledges the cognitive needs of students (Butler, Marsh, Slavinsky, & Baraniuk, 2014). The influence of multimedia on instructional design, learning management systems, and interactive multimedia-based learning changes the culture of the classroom from a space where students sit and listen to the teacher to an interactive space where students engage with each other and the teacher in multifaceted learning modalities that shape cognition and evolve human interaction skills.

Schrader (2016), in examining the impact of multimedia, notes that "[C]ollege age students and younger students exhibit numerous and important differences when learning from multimedia content" (p. 1). As multimedia-mediated content (both auditory/verbal and visual knowledge)[1] is incorporated into the learning experience, the multimedia presentation enriches the learning instruction more effectively than presenting through a single medium in rote learning, so the students can obtain the information in a more meaningful way and repeatedly through different media and choices (Dembo & Seli, 2012).

The learner engaged in multimedia learning, as Mayer (2002, 2009) explains, is focused on the auditory/verbal channel and the visual channel of cognition, and it is this dual channel perspective of instruction and learning that enriches the classroom experience.[2] Equally important, the use of multiple channels can increase the amount of information that the learner's brain can process (Sweller, 2005a).

Well-designed multimedia learning affords two outcomes: multimedia learning can enable learners to come to understandings more quickly than through more conventional classroom or textual media; and perhaps equal, if not more significant, multimedia learning can change how the learner comes to know or to understand and hence *what* the learner knows and understands. In other words, a learner may have an image or a mental "construction" that is far richer than an abstract verbal understanding. From an educational perspective, it is essential that learners can move confidently between concrete and abstract understandings and not become locked into one or the other (Mayer & Massa, 2003).

THE INFLUENCE OF MULTIMEDIA LEARNING ON THE CLASSROOM

The learning culture of teaching and learning experiences in P–12 and higher education classrooms has shifted paradigms from predominantly instructor-focused pedagogies to learner-centered pedagogies (Hsu & Wolfe, 2003; Yamauchi, 2008). The shift in paradigms is a result of advances in technology-infused curriculum and instruction: instructional systems and advanced use of Web-based and digital technologies have created new learning spaces and opportunities for both the instructor and the student. "Effective multimedia projects demonstrate alignment or a clear connection between the content, activities, and assessments" (Frey & Sutton, 2010, p. 496).

Although educators have seen a constant evolution in the methods and technologies used in concert to design and deliver instruction, how individuals learn has remained constant; what has changed is our understanding of how individuals learn. Mayer's (2009) cognitive theory of multimedia learning presents the idea that the brain does not interpret a multimedia presentation of words, pictures, and auditory information in a mutually exclusive fashion; rather, these elements are selected and organized dynamically to produce logical mental constructs.

Multimedia learning instructional sources may be simulations, games, puzzles, problem-based learning activities, tutorials, presentations, animations, case studies, or assessments. The format of a learning activity or experience depends on the learning goals and resources used to meet the learners' needs and modalities of learning (Frey & Sutton, 2010; Mayer, 2009).

Multimedia learning activities or learning experiences are "those that integrate media objects such as text, graphics, video, animation, and sound to represent and convey information [which have] the potential to connect key learning objectives in a prescribed curriculum to real[-]world contexts, integrate diverse curriculum areas, support student decision-making, and foster authentic collaboration" (Crichton & Kopp, 2006, para. 4).

Multimedia allow teachers to integrate text, graphics, animation, and other media into one interfaced set of information and to present comprehensive information for their students to achieve specified course outcomes (Mayer, 2003, 2009). Multimedia permit the demonstration of complicated processes in a highly interactive, animated fashion and enable instructional material to be interconnected with other related topics in a more natural and intuitive way (Frey & Sutton, 2010).

Whereas specific content presented in a multimedia activity or learning experience is important, it is equally important to understand that the design of learning material requires attention to cognitive functioning and cognitive load[3] in the individual learner. Each learner functions differently in terms of cognition and modalities of learning; the verbal versus visual learner integrates knowledge differently into existing schema.[4]

Likewise, each learner has a different cognitive load factor in terms of how much he is able to assimilate cognitively. Clark and Mayer (2003) note that one of the challenges of multimedia learning projects "is to build lessons in ways that are compatible with human learning processes. To be effective, instructional methods must support these processes. That is, they must foster the psychological events necessary for learning" (p. 30).

THE INFLUENCE OF MULTIMEDIA LEARNING PRINCIPLES ON INSTRUCTION

Sweller (2005b) states that "good instructional design is driven by our knowledge of human cognitive structures and the manner in which those structures are organized" (p. 19). Designing multimedia instruction[5] requires understanding that "construction of knowledge is constrained by the learner's working memory (WM) capacity and learning processes (e.g., attending to relevant incoming information)" (Greer, Crutchfield, & Woods, 2013, p. 42). With respect to designing multimedia instruction, three assumptions about how individuals learn must be taken into account: dual channel assumption, limited processing capacity assumption, and active processing assumption (Mayer, 2009).

The *dual channel assumption* means that individuals possess two channels for processing information: auditory/verbal material and visual material, or what the learner sees and hears (Mayer, 2003, 2005, 2008). Designing multimedia instruction requires considering the knowledge of how people learn when they are developing a learning session or environment by presenting the material in both auditory/verbal and visual form. The dual channel assumption applied to instruction ensures that each learner's modality of learning and how he learns are considered.

The *limited processing capacity assumption* means that individuals are limited in the amount of information that can be processed in each channel at one time. Research shows that humans have a relatively small average memory span—approximately five to seven chunks—plus or minus two (Sorden, 2005, 2013; Sweller, 2005a). Designing multimedia learning instruction and activities uses this knowledge of limited capacity to make important decisions about the amount of content shown to learners at one time.

The *active processing assumption* means that individuals actively engage in cognitive processing in order to construct a coherent mental representation of their experiences. When designers of multimedia learning use this knowledge of active processing, they focus on how to ensure that learners are paying attention to the right information and organizing the incoming knowledge (Mayer, 2008, 2009; Sorden, 2013). Instructional design also requires a focus on how to help the learners integrate the incoming information with what they already know. Instructional design of multimedia learning requires care when deciding how to actively engage the learner with the content presented.

Classroom instruction for multimedia learning involves a set of principles that can be applied for the instructional design of multimedia messages or presentations to be used in the classroom. The set includes twelve principles:

1. *Multimedia Principle*: Students learn better from words and pictures than from words alone. Providing two channels of information for learning improves the opportunity for learning and acknowledges the different learning needs and modalities of individual learners.

2. *Spatial Contiguity Principle*: Students learn better when corresponding words and pictures are presented near rather than far from each other on the page or screen. Keeping corresponding words and pictures close together reduces cognitive load by reducing the mental effort needed to scan and search the page or screen and allows both to be held in the working memory at the same time.
3. *Temporal Contiguity Principle*: Students learn better when corresponding words and pictures are presented simultaneously rather than successively. When the visual (animation/image) and the auditory/verbal (narration/words) are presented to the learner at different times, it is more difficult for the learner to create mental representations, and the working memory is quickly overloaded. Presenting the animation and narration (or text and image) to the learner at the same time is important.
4. *Coherence Principle*: Students learn better when extraneous words, pictures, and sounds are excluded rather than included. The learning experience is enriched through instructional design when interesting but irrelevant words, pictures, sounds, music, and symbols are eliminated from the lesson.
5. *Signaling Principle*: Students learn better when cues that highlight the organization of the essential material are added. Inserting cues that direct the learner's attention toward the essential material (visual and auditory/verbal) is key to reducing extraneous processing or cognitive overload.
6. *Modality Principle*: Students learn better from a combination of animation and narration than from animation and on-screen text. The use of pictures and printed words overloads the visual channel of the cognitive processing system and reduces learning. Using spoken words offloads the visual channel and makes excellent use of the auditory channel, reducing cognitive overload.
7. *Personalization Principle*: Students learn better from multimedia lessons when words are in conversational style rather than formal style. Personalization involves using "you" and "your" in the narration rather than "the." Learners are more likely to try harder and engage at a deeper level when they see the author as a conversational partner.
8. *Redundancy Principle*: Students learn better from animation and narration than from animation, narration, and on-screen text. Redundancy creates cognitive overload by having to visually scan between pictures and on-screen text, which can tire the learner mentally.
9. *Segmenting Principle*: Students learn better from a multimedia lesson presented in user-paced segments rather than as a continuous unit. When presenting learners with a series of steps to a process, it is best to break the lesson into smaller steps so the learner can grasp one step before

moving on to the next. This allows the learner to control when to move to the next step.
10. *Individual Differences Principle*: Design effects are stronger for low-knowledge learners than for high-knowledge learners and for high-spatial learners rather than for low-spatial learners.
11. *Image Principle*: Students do not necessarily learn better from a multimedia lesson when the speaker's voice is added to the screen. This includes the use of pedagogical agents or characters.
12. *Voice Principle*: Students learn better when the narration in multimedia lessons is spoken in a friendly human voice rather than in a machine voice. It gives a sense that someone is talking directly to the learner. (Adapted from Mayer, 2009)

Designing multimedia lessons and related presentations for the classroom requires that the instructor focus on the principles and the underlying multimedia learning theory that are the basis for the principles.

The full set of principles applies to any format of multimedia instruction; however, they are especially important in the context of digital and computer technologies-based and related media learning. This is important because in order to construct knowledge and develop understanding, "learners are exposed to material in verbal (such as on-screen text or narration) as well as pictorial form (including static materials such as photos or illustrations, and dynamic materials such as video or animation)" (Mayer & Moreno, 2002, pp. 87–88).

THE INFLUENCE OF MULTIMEDIA LEARNING ON THE FORMS AND NATURE OF KNOWLEDGE

As multimedia and digital technologies become more integrated into the classroom and instruction, it is important to ask to what extent, if at all, such developments change the forms and nature of knowledge.

Teaching and learning are two complementary aspects of education. Learning includes two key elements: content, which forms the "what" of learning; and skills, which describe the application of content to specific tasks, or the "how." These two elements are mirrored in teaching by the curriculum and content (the "what") and the instruction (the "how"). Multimedia learning technologies affect both aspects of teaching and learning in three ways: how they present information; how students interact both *with* the medium and *through* the medium with the teacher and other learners; and how knowledge is structured within multimedia.

Mayer's Cognitive Theory of Multimedia Learning (Mayer, 2005; Mayer & Moreno, 2002) posits that multimedia narration (auditory/verbal) and graphic images (visual) produce verbal and visual mental representations, which integrate with prior knowledge in existing schemas to construct new knowledge. First, an individual's working memory includes auditory and visual channels. Second, each subschema of working memory has a limited capacity, consistent with Cognitive Load Theory (Sweller, 2005a). Third, individuals are knowledge-constructing processors who produce meaningful learning when they attend to relevant incoming information, organize the information in coherent representational structures, and then integrate it with other existing knowledge (Mayer, 2005). Fourth, connections can be made only if corresponding visual and auditory/verbal representations are in working memory at the same time (Sorden, 2013).

Sweller (2005a explains that the Cognitive Theory of Multimedia Learning includes three memory stores known as sensory memory, working memory, and long-term memory.

1. *Sensory memory* is the cognitive structure that permits us to perceive new information.
2. *Working memory* is the cognitive structure in which we consciously process information.
3. *Long-term memory* is the cognitive structure that stores our knowledge base.

We are only conscious of information in long-term memory when it has been transferred to working memory.

As individuals experience a multimedia learning instruction message or presentation, the visual and auditory/verbal knowledge is introduced into the existing memory. Whereas sensory memory store briefly holds pictures and printed text as visual images, and auditory memory briefly holds spoken words and sounds as auditory images, working memory attends to or selects information from sensory memory for processing and integration. Long-term memory holds the entire store of a person's knowledge for an indefinite amount of time (Mayer, 2005; Sweller, 2005b).

In addition to the three memory stores, five forms of representation of words/text (auditory/verbal) and pictures (visual) occur as information that is processed by memory and sequenced into the three memory stores (Mayer, 2005). Each form represents a particular stage of processing in the three different memory stores:

1. The first form of representation is words and pictures in the multimedia instruction message or presentation itself.

2. The second form is the acoustic representation (sounds) and iconic representation (images) in sensory memory.
3. The third form is the sounds and images in working memory.
4. The fourth form of representation is the verbal and pictorial models, which are also found in working memory.
5. The fifth form is prior knowledge, or *schemas*, which are stored in long-term memory (Sorden, 2013).

THE INFLUENCE OF MULTIMEDIA LITERACY ON LEARNING

Literacy in math, reading, writing, and related disciplines has dominated education for generations. With the advance of digital technologies and multimedia infused in society, teaching and learning are now confronted with the need to rethink the types of literacies important to the classroom. The metaphor of multimedia literacy provides one means of imagining a more coherent and ambitious approach that acknowledges the place of digital technologies and multimedia that are infused in students at an early age (Tan & Guo, 2009).

The increasing convergence of contemporary media with digital technologies means that we need to address the skills and competencies—the multimedia and digital literacies—that are required by the whole range of rapidly expanding contemporary forms of communication (visual and verbal alike). The concept of multimedia literacies represents use of diverse media—visual, audio, gestural, spatial, and tactile dimensions of communication—in addition to traditional written and oral forms (Cope & Kalantzis, 2009).

Leu, Kinzer, Coiro, and Cammack (2004), writing on new literacies emerging from the internet and other information and communication technologies, note that the new literacies for the twenty-first century can be succinctly defined as follows:

> The new literacies of the Internet and other ICTs [information and communication technologies] include the skills, strategies, and dispositions necessary to successfully use and adapt to the rapidly changing information and communication technologies and contexts that continuously emerge in our world and influence all areas of our personal and professional lives. These new literacies allow us to use the Internet and other ICTs to identify important questions, locate information, critically evaluate the usefulness of that information, synthesize information to answer those questions, and then communicate the answers to others. (p. 1572)

Multimedia literacy involves a "rigorous analysis of media texts, in terms of the visual and verbal languages they employ and the representations of the world they make available" (Buckingham, 2007, p. 14). Multimedia literacy is a concern for both the educator and the student.

The educator engaging in use of multimedia instruction will need a high level of multimedia literacy, particularly as she introduces multimedia learning activities into the classroom. Equally important, the student entering the classroom in schools and universities already, to some extent, has a level of media and digital technologies literacy. Ensuring that students have a level of multimedia literacy essential to engaging in multimedia learning activities and experiences is key to successful multimedia teaching and learning.

Society has moved from a culture of "telling the world to showing the world" (Kress, 2003, p. 140). Educators in this multimedia age are confronted with the need to shift to multimedia literacies as a form of "shorthand for the myriad social practices and conceptions of engaging in meaning making mediated by texts that are produced, received, distributed, exchanged, etc.[,] via digital codification" (Lankshear & Knobel, 2008, p. 5).

These multimedia-based sources of knowledge present a dual channel (visual and verbal) cognitive load (e.g., images, animation, movies, podcasts, blogs, and online social networking sites) that encodes knowledge very differently for the educator and the student. Lotherington and Jenson (2011) are instructive when they argue that "both what is produced and how one knows and comes to know are different from these processes in traditional print-based literacies" (p. 230).

CONCLUSIONS

New technologies—digital, Web-based, and media-based—are fundamentally changing the nature of education, both K–12 and higher education. With that in mind, we need to maintain a balance between face-to-face teaching and learning and media- and technology-based teaching and learning. The skills necessary to function and grow in a digital-age, multimedia-enriched society cannot or should not be taught solely through media- and digital technology-based instruction; now and always the need will be for the more humanizing experience of teaching and learning in the face-to-face setting.

The important consideration in multimedia-based teaching and learning is to recognize that design of multimedia instruction is concerned with the alignment of content and instruction with the learning needs and modalities of the new generation of students growing up in a vastly different world due to Web 2.0 and digital technologies. The teacher and the student now interface through multimedia instructional messages and presentations that represent both visual and auditory/verbal sources of knowledge. Equally important is the consideration that the teacher is also a learner in this classroom environment enriched with multimedia.

The ideal classroom of the future will be one in which the roles of teacher, learner, and multimedia and digital technologies are all in balance and complement one another. Teachers and learners will become more concerned with the management of knowledge than with mastery of all areas. The teacher's role will combine guidance on appropriate areas of knowledge and subject matter with the generation of new knowledge and the application of that knowledge. The learner's role will be to evolve multimedia literacies essential to functioning in a rapidly evolving media- and technology-enriched society.

The multimedia role will be to interface the teacher and learner with visual and verbal knowledge, through carefully designed multimedia presentations that acknowledge the differences in learning modalities of the learner. Above all, the teacher's role will be to challenge and stimulate the learner to engage in collaborative, creative, and critical inquiry.

NOTES

1. Mayer's (2009) research focused on the cognition and multimedia learning focused on the three primary assumptions:

    1. Visual and auditory experiences or information are processed through separate and distinct information processing "channels."
    2. Each information-processing channel is limited in its ability to process experiences or information.
    3. Processing experiences or information in the channels is an active process designed to construct coherent mental representations.

2. Mayer (2009) explains the five steps of processing involved in the cognitive theory of multimedia learning: (1) selecting relevant words, (2) selecting relevant images, (3) organizing selected words, (4) organizing selected images, and (5) integrating verbal and visual representation as well as prior knowledge.

3. Research on cognitive load states that working memory is limited in its capacity to selectively attend to and process incoming sensory data (Sorden, 2005, 2013; Sweller, 2005a, 2005b; Sweller, Van Merriënboer, & Paas, 1998). Cognitive load theory is concerned with the way in which a learner's cognitive resources are focused and used during learning and problem solving, suggesting that for instruction to be effective, care must be taken to design instruction in a way that does not overload the mind's capacity for processing information.

4. Mayer (2002, 2003, 2009), in his research on multimedia learning theory, explains that the cognitive theory of multimedia learning addresses the competing nature of the dual channels (auditory and visual) for processing information in the

construction of knowledge in contrast to basic information delivery theory, which focuses on the methods of delivery (e.g., audio, video, text).

5. Multimedia instructional design, as used here, refers to "the entire process of analysis of learning needs and goals and the development of a delivery system to meet those needs" and includes "development of instructional materials and activities; and tryout and evaluation of all instruction and learner activities" (University of Michigan, 1996, p. 1).

REFERENCES

Buckingham, D. (2007). *Schooling the digital generation: Popular culture, new media and the future of education.* London, UK: UCL IOE Press.

Butler, A. C., Marsh, E. J., Slavinsky, J. P., & Baraniuk, R. G. (2014). Integrating cognitive science and technology improves learning in a STEM classroom. *Educational Psychology Review, 26,* 331–340.

Clark, R. C., & Mayer, R. E. (2003). *e-Learning and the science of instruction.* San Francisco, CA: Pfeiffer.

Clarke, R. Y. (2012). *The next-generation classroom: Smart, interactive and connected learning environments.* White paper sponsored by Samsung. Alexandria, VA: IDC Government Insights.

Cope, B., & Kalantzis, M. (2009). A grammar of multimodality. *International Journal of Learning. 16,* 361–425. doi:10.1080/15544800903076044.

Crichton, S., & Kopp, G. (2006). Multimedia technologies, multiple intelligences, and teacher professional development in an international education project. *Innovative Online, 2*(3). Retrieved from http://www.innovateonline.info/pdf/vol2_issue3/Multimedia_Technologies,_Multiple_Intelligences,_and_Teacher_Professional_Development_in_an_International_Education_Project.pdf.

Dembo, M. H., & Seli, H. (2012). *Motivation and learning strategies for college success: A focus on self-regulated learning.* New York, NY: Erlbaum.

Frey, B. A., & Sutton, J. M. (2010). A model for developing multimedia learning projects. *MERLOT Journal of Online Learning and Teaching, 6*(2), 49–507.

Greer, D. L., Crutchfield, S. A., & Woods, K. L. (2013). Cognitive theory of multimedia learning, instructional design principles, and students with learning disabilities in computer-based and online learning environments. *Technology in Education, 193*(2), 4150.

Hsu, C. H. C., & Wolfe, K. (2003). Learning styles of hospitality students and faculty members. *Journal of Hospitality & Tourism Education, 14*(3), 19–27.

Kozma, R. B. (1991). Learning with media. *Review of Educational Research, 61,* 179–211.

Kozma, R. B. (1994). The influence of media on learning: The debate continues. *SLMQ, 22*(4). Retrieved from http://www.ala.org/aasl/sites/ala.org.aasl/files/content/aaslpubsandjournals/slr/edchoice/SLMQ_InfluenceofMediaonLearning_InfoPower.pdf.

Kress, G. (2003). *Literacy in the new media age.* London, UK: Routledge.
Lankshear, C., & Knobel, M. (2006). *New literacies: Everyday practices and classroom learning.* Maidenhead, UK: McGraw Hill/Open University Press.
Leu, D. J., Jr., Kinzer, C. K., Coiro, J. L., & Cammack, D. W. (2004). Towards a theory of new literacies emerging from the Internet and other information and communication technologies. In R. B. Ruddell & N. J. Unrau (Eds.), *Theoretical models and processes of reading* (5th ed., pp. 1570–1613). Newark, DE: International Reading Association.
Lotherington, H., & Jenson, J. (2011). Teaching multimodal and digital literacy in L2 settings: New literacies, new basics, new pedagogies. *Annual Review of Applied Linguistics, 31*, 226–246.
Mayer, R. E. (2002). Cognitive theory and the design of multimedia instruction: An example of the two-way street between cognition and instruction. *New Directions for Teaching and Learning, 89*, 55–71.
Mayer, R. E. (2003). The promise of multimedia learning: Using the same instructional design methods across different media. *Learning and Instruction, 12*, 125–139.
Mayer, R. E. (2005). Cognitive theory of multimedia learning. In R. E. Mayer (Ed.), *The Cambridge handbook of multimedia learning* (pp. 31–48). Cambridge, UK: Cambridge University Press.
Mayer, R. E. (2008). *Learning and instruction* (2nd ed.). Upper Saddle River, NY: Pearson Merrill Prentice Hall.
Mayer, R. E. (2009). *Multimedia learning* (2nd ed.). New York, NY: Cambridge University Press.
Mayer, R. E., Hegarty, M., Mayer, S., & Cambel, J. (2005). When static media promote active learning: Annotated illustrations versus narrated animations in multimedia instruction. *Journal of Experimental Psychology: Applied, 11*(4), 256–265.
Mayer, R. E., & Massa, L. J. (2003). Three facets of visual and verbal learners: Cognitive ability, cognitive style, and learning preference. *Journal of Educational Psychology, 4*, 833–846. doi:10.1037/0022-0663.95.4.833.
Mayer, R., & Moreno, R. (2002). Animation as an aid to multimedia learning. *Educational Psychology Review, 14*(1), 87–99.
Reed, S. K. (2006). Cognitive architectures for multimedia learning. *Educational Psychologist, 41*(2), 87–98.
Schrader, P. G. (2016). Does multimedia theory apply to all students? The impact of multimedia presentations on science learning. *Journal of Learning and Teaching in Digital Age (JOLTIDA), 1*(1). Retrieved from http://www.joltida.org/index.php/joltida/rt/printerFriendly/8/90.
Sorden, S. D. (2005). A cognitive approach to instructional design for multimedia learning. *Informing Science Journal, 8*, 263–278.
Sorden, S. D. (2013). The cognitive theory of multimedia learning. In B. J. Irby, G. Brown, R. Lara-Alecio, & S. H. Jackson (Eds.), *Handbook of educational theories* (pp. 155–168). Charlotte, NC: Information Age Publishing.

Sweller, J. (2005a). Implications of cognitive load theory for multimedia learning. In R. E. Mayer (Ed.), *The Cambridge handbook of multimedia learning* (pp. 27–42). New York, NY: Cambridge University Press.

Sweller, J. (2005b). The redundancy principle in multimedia learning. In R.E. Mayer (Ed.), *The Cambridge handbook of multimedia learning* (pp. 159–167). New York, NY: Cambridge University Press.

Sweller, J., Van Merriënboer, J. J. G., & Paas, F. G. W. C. (1998). Cognitive architecture and instructional design. *Educational Psychology Review, 10*(3), 251–229.

Tan, L., & Guo, L. (2009). From print to critical multimedia literacy: One teacher's foray into new literacies practices. *Journal of Adolescent & Adult Literacy, 53*(4), 315–324.

University of Michigan. (1996). Definitions of instructional design. Retrieved from http://www.umich.edu/~ed626/define.html.

Chapter 5

The New Generation of Students

Abbey N. Boorman

INTRODUCTION

Today's generation has been called many different names: Net Generation or Net Gen (Tapscott, 1998; Oblinger & Oblinger, 2005), Digital Natives (Prensky, 2001), iGeneration (Rosen, 2007), Homo Zappiens (Veen & Vrakking, 2006), Generation Z (Gen Z) and post-Millennials (Dimock, 2018), to name some of the most popular. All of these terms have been used to varying levels of condescension, reverence, despondency, and optimism. This chapter will examine today's generation of students as related to media and digital technology use.

GEN Z

In an effort to use a more neutral term, Gen Z will be used primarily in this chapter to refer to those born after the year 1997. This term applies to current young professionals, students in college, and students in K–12 schools. Millennials and Gen Z are similar in that their lives were heavily influenced by their increased use of digital technology, the internet, and social media, but the frequency and manner in which they engage in multimedia have created a significant generational difference that demands immediate attention.

Increasingly, educators have come to an understanding of these changes and adapted their pedagogies and classroom resources. In an effort to shift school from teacher-directed instruction to learner-centered instruction, policy makers have initiated education standards that require the use of multimedia and technology in instruction as learner-centered tools. Today, multimedia is primarily exercised digitally through various digital mediums, and multimedia learning is a process of communication and creation, rather than solely of consumption. In a common educational practice Larry Cuban (2001) describes as "oversold and underused," school administrators often purchase technology for technology's sake, due to increasing pressure to integrate classrooms, without consideration of how it might be used and the type of technological device that would be best to attain certain goals. The result of this type of decision making is a technology-centered approach to instruction rather than optimal learner-centered instruction. According to Richard Mayer (2009), the primary issue of technology-centered instruction is that "the focus [is] on giving people access to the latest technology rather than on helping people to learn through the aid of technology" (p. 12).

Moreover, teachers often are not provided adequate training on how to use these devices in the classroom. Consequently, the devices are not used often, and teachers resort to traditional teacher-directed instructor controlling the entire curriculum and methods of instruction. With less ability to vary multimedia, teachers become limited to those available in print media and the teacher's computer and projection device. Because of common misunderstandings of implementing changes to ensure learner-centered instruction, it is imperative that educators understand how current multimedia consumption and creation have impacted how Gen Z and future generations learn and work in and out of the classroom (Barnes, Marateo, & Ferris, 2007; Glendinning, 2018). Understanding the Gen Z experiences and educational needs will help guide better choices regarding curriculum, instruction, assessment, allocation of funds for classroom resources, school infrastructure, future education policies, and teacher training.

THE ELEPHANT IN THE ROOM: MILLENNIALS VERSUS GEN Z

Generational eras are not defined formally by any government agency, but the titles of generations can be used as a tool to identify trends in culture and allow for other types of analyses like the ones in this chapter (Dimock, 2018). Although Millennials (born between 1981 and 1996) often are portrayed by the later generations as nearly synonymous with Gen Zers, the life of a person born after 1996 has been markedly different and impacted by the social and economic events of that time, a fact that cannot be discounted or devalued in any related analyses. Despite the primary connection between Millennials and technological advancement, the internet was not made commercially available until 1995, when the earliest Millennials were teenagers. In addition, the newest functions of cellular phones were its increased mobility outside the car, the diminishing size and weight, the increased affordability and expansion of cellular service, and, later, the ability to use text messaging. Social media were born in this generation (and created predominantly by Millennials) with blogging and early social media platforms of the late 1990s and first decade of the 2000s, such as MySpace and LinkedIn. At the same time, although many Millennials may not have had home access to high-speed internet, mobile phones, or social media during their formative years, Gen Zers do not know a world without these innovations.

It is also important to acknowledge that most Gen Z lives are recorded or documented early on social media platforms such as Facebook and, later, Instagram and Snapchat. More data are collected through an individual's online activity from companies such as Google, Amazon, and Facebook. About young people's activity on social media, Palfrey and Gasser (2016) claim, "The new effect of the digital age—paradoxically—is a potential decrease in a person's ability to control her social identity and how others perceive her" (p. 20). Although the full impact and results of being raised in such surveillance are only speculative at this point, Gen Z mostly likely will face the consequences of not having a protected right to privacy more than any other generation before it.

Beyond technological advancements, Gen Z has been affected by a volatile U.S. economy and social justice movements (Seemiller & Grace, 2017). Gen Z was shaped by the economic turmoil of the Great Recession; the xenophobia and Islamophobia of post-9/11 and the War on Terror; and the social justice movements for the rights of African Americans, LGBTQ, women, and immigrants. Further, Gen Z in particular has been victimized by the widespread frequency and "normalcy" of school shootings and violence post-Columbine, living in a culture of pervasive fear and outrage at the questioned safety of American schools. It is, therefore, unfair and wholly inaccurate to conclude that these two generations may have equal points of comparison in culture, knowledge, learning preferences, or workplace training, despite some of the common characteristics the two share.

GEN Z AND THE AGE OF INFORMATION

In *The Information Behavior of a New Generation: Children and Teens in the 21st Century*, contributing authors Abbas and Agosto (2013) argue, "[Today's generation] encounter the same issues that young people have always dealt with, but now they have more sources and channels of information in which to find help with their everyday life information needs" (p. 86). In order to understand the predominant characteristics of Gen Z, it is vital to explore the nature and impact of growing information sources available to them. Popular sources of information include social media platforms such as Facebook, Instagram, and Snapchat; search engines such as Google; online news articles; news outlets via streaming, cable, or radio services; unofficial sources such as podcasts, blogs, vlogs, and wikis; and books, either electronic or print. The ability to communicate information is not limited by boundaries like time or space that restricted most information sources before new technologies (Collins & Halverson, 2009). Further, despite having a reputation for being egocentric and apathetic to the learning process, Gen Zers engage in information-seeking activity daily through multimedia on their own and value the knowledge of their efforts more than the information gained from "a teacher explaining the world as it is according to him/her" (Veen & Vrakking, 2006, p. 10).

Gen Zers are not only collecting information in new ways, but the manner in which they engage with information is as new as the media they use. Researchers have identified the unique quality of current information-seeking activity:

> Classically, reasoning has been concerned with the deductive and abstract. But our observation of kids working with digital media suggests *bricolage* to use more than abstract logic . . . It has to do with abilities to find something—an object, tool, document, a piece of code—and to use it to build something you deem important. (Brown, 2000, p. 14)

Accordingly, skills related to finding information are more relevant and valuable for this generation than the memorization skills that were required of previous generations in school. Palfrey and Gasser (2016), researchers from Harvard's Berkman Klein Center for Internet and Society, identify the actions of young people engaging in digital information as a three-step process: first, *grazing*; second, *deep-diving*; and third, engaging in *feedback loops*. By engaging in these activities, information is not limited to consumption, but it also may be shared with others or created from their own experiences and knowledge.

The first step of gathering information, *grazing*, is a process in which information is consumed through short lines of text and from media that are easily accessible, quick to process, and organized well (Palfrey & Gasser, 2016, p. 207). Examples of these sources might be videos or hypertexts shared on social media on a person's phone or tablet, or a search for information on Google from a computer or phone using a basic keyword search. During the *deep-dive* stage, the person uses critical thinking skills in determining the credibility of the source of information; and instead of valuing speed and accessibility, the key factors in this consumption and learning process are "accuracy, trustworthiness, insight, analysis, new angles, and relationships"

(Palfrey & Gasser, 2016, p. 208). Finally, the last stage, in which the person is ready to interact with the information, the *feedback loop* involves sharing the information with others and/or commenting on it. It occurs when people share hyperlinks, videos, or images with text on social media or when users comment on Facebook statuses, tweets, or Instagram stories. It also occurs on wikis, online bulletin boards, comment sections of blogs, videos, or news articles. Variation in the way people engage in this stage resides in the user's discretion of the validity of the information and the use of appropriate media for certain types of information (Palfrey & Gasser, 2016).

On one side, this type of interaction with information is the source of internet scams, false information or "fake news," and perceptions of negative and inauthentic human interaction with real-world consequences. Criticisms of Gen Z use of social media, text messages, and the camera on phones are rampant. In his book *The Dumbest Generation*, Michael Bauerlein (2008) displays a common viewpoint that Gen Z students are losing essential real-life skills that previous generations had to use and are increasingly egocentric:

> Teen images and songs, hot gossip and games, and youth-to-youth communications no longer limited by time or space wrap them up in a generational cocoon ... The autonomy has a cost: the most they attend to themselves, the less they remember the past and envision a future. They have all the advantages of modernity and democracy, but when the gifts of life lead to social joys, not intellectual labor, the minds of the young plateau at age 18. (p. 10)

On the other hand, educators today have a unique ability to take a more positive position on Gen Z media use and habits. Their form of interaction with information provides opportunities for relevant application of critical-thinking skills and literacy that are vital, powerful learning tools for students today. Educators must examine the perspectives, habits, strengths, and deficits of Gen Z in order to help the generation become citizens who bolster economic and social achievement in the world they already are helping to create.

GEN Z IN THE CLASSROOM

As previously demonstrated, Gen Z students in the classroom are still characteristically aligned with their culture as producers and consumers of media, yet often they are operating in classrooms more aligned with traditional methods of schooling familiar to generations before them. They come to the classroom with self- and peer-taught information-processing skills, technical ability, and social justice imperatives that are not necessarily modeled or taught in their formal education (Prensky, 2001). Seemiller and Grace (2017) assert, "Generation Z students believe that that they have the power to change the world" (p. 22). However, they do not view that powerful agency as being endorsed by the traditional education system.

This generation's type of reasoning is not conducive to teacher-directed instruction and demands for memorization of information. The accessibility of information has not rendered the need for memorization skills obsolete, but it has made them less vital compared to other processing skills. The consequence of this dissonance between what they need and what they are getting is engendering negative results. According to researchers Barnes, Marateo, and Ferris (2007), "Accustomed as they are to multiple stimuli, Net Geners report being bored in the traditional classroom" (p. 3). Instead, they generally report a desire for curriculum and instruction that can be customized to their particular interests, goals, strengths, and deficits. The characteristics, perspectives, and skills of the Gen Z students should not be perceived as worthless; on the contrary, it is how they are being used and treated in the classroom that is antithetical to truly educating and meeting the needs of this generation.

MULTIMEDIA IN THE CLASSROOM

In an interview with the *New York Dramatic Mirror* in 1913 on the topic of motion pictures, Thomas Edison famously claimed, "Books will soon be obsolete in the public schools. Scholars will be instructed through the eye" (Smith, 1913, p. 24). Although books have not been proven obsolete in the classroom, the increase in the availability and variability of multimedia, including film and video, has greatly impacted traditional instruction. Students are instructed not only through the eye, as Edison claimed, but also through touch, sound, and kinesthetics. On the history of using media in the classroom, Larry Cuban (1986) writes:

> Chalk and slate, books and pictures were nineteenth-century media used to expand the sole medium of instruction—teacher talk—into a broader array of visual tools for conveying facts, skills, and values. More recently, films, radio, tape recorders, television, and computers have entered the teacher's cupboard to be counted as automated and electronic teacher helpers. (pp. 3–4)

Since Cuban's research in the 1980s, the internet and technological devices have clearly made available even more multimedia sources for students and educators. Despite the availability of resources and decades of research asserting the value of multimedia in instruction, multimedia learning is not being exercised in every classroom with maximum efficiency. Reasons for this disconnect include educators' lack of appropriate training and support in using varied forms of multimedia and technology and creating a learner-centered classroom environment, prevailing pessimistic views of instructional technologies and student media activities outside the classroom, and a lack of understanding of the current literacy and critical-thinking skills necessary for Gen Z students.

Lately, technology has become synonymous with media as the most popular media may be made available through the latest technological devices. However, as previously mentioned, technology often is provided by administrators with little care for choosing appropriate devices and software for particular learning needs, leading to technology being widely "oversold and underused" by teachers and students (Cuban, 2001). Research has demonstrated that technology integration in the classroom has been impacted by "the top three barriers—resources (40 percent), knowledge and skills (23 percent), attitude and beliefs (13 percent)—[which] made up for 76 percent of those mentioned in current literature" (Blocher, et al., 2011, p. 158). Even though most teachers who have entered the field in the past decade have a better chance of having some technological skills, those skills are not necessarily transferring into their pedagogy (Ertmer & Ottenbreit-Leftwich, 2010; Kim, et al., 2013). At the same time, being a technology user does not necessarily indicate a belief that the use of multimedia or technology benefit student learning (Vatanartiran & Karadeniz, 2015), and many teachers may suffer anxiety over the appropriateness of using technology in the classroom (Tapscott, 1999). Moreover, as noted by An and Reigeluth (2011), "It is possible that teachers who are learner-centered in philosophy are teacher-centered in actual practice" (p. 60).

In order for educators to meet the needs of Gen Z students and to increase learner-centered instruction, it will require what Brown (2000) describes as "a shift between using technology to support the individual to using technology to support relationships between individuals" (p. 20). Extending this concept specifically to include multimedia learning, Mayer (2009) claims that a learner-centered approach focuses on "multimedia technology as an aid to human cognition" (p. 13). This type of instruction requires an additional shift from teacher as the expert in the room who is responsible for dispersing the information to the students to teacher as a facilitator of information, mentor in learning, and teacher of critical skills. In a learner-centered classroom, the learning tends to be more constructivist and participatory in nature, allowing the student more control and agency in his own learning. This type of learning has the additional benefit of increasing student engagement (Bebell & Kay, 2010) and using agency as active in the learning process (Mayer, 2009) rather than experiencing it as a passive position.

The myth of the skills and knowledge "digital natives" has been repeatedly debunked in practice and theory (Kirschner & Bruyckere, 2017). Even if students use technology and media in their daily lives, educators cannot use that fact to make assumptions about their skills level. In a contributing chapter of *Dancing with Digital Natives* (2011), Bell astutely recognizes,

> While it is true that digital natives have a great degree of comfort with technology, it must be remembered that they do not know everything about it. . . . Failure on the part of parents, educators, employers, and others in leadership positions to provide guidance and instruction is a woeful abdication of responsibility. (p. 356)

Therefore, students will need to be educated on how to use media in a practical and ethical sense. Just as we teach young ones how to be polite in public and use basic good manners in face-to-face interaction, students today must learn how to interact online appropriately. In addition, participants and creators of media bear a responsibility to use good judgment and discernment in their consumption and dissemination of information across media.

A new type of student is born through the circular consumption and creation of media, leading to a more globalized culture; participants who use communication and critical-thinking skills go beyond our current conception of writing, reading, and speaking. Howard Gardner, father of the theory of multiple intelligences, asserts the need of certain minds, or skills, that will be necessary to cultivate in the future: *the disciplined mind, the synthesizing mind, the creating mind, the respectful mind,* and *the ethical mind* (Gardner, 2010). All of these minds or skills are related to how people gain, use, and promote information. In the age of information, advanced types of communication skills are critical. The time for educators to rethink education with future and current students in mind already has begun (Glendinning, 2018).

IMPLICATIONS FOR EDUCATIONAL LEADERS

Overall, Gen Zers have demonstrated that they want to succeed and do well in school (Barnes, Marateo, & Ferris, 2005), and educators should not interpret their activity in the digital realm as apathy or disengagement with their education. Rather, educators should help fuel and develop their skills and passions to maximize their impact. Moreover, "educators should continue to find ways to exploit the skills students develop outside of class without accommodating the habits of instant gratification and shallow thinking" (Barnes,

Marateo, & Ferris, 2007, p. 6). Enacting this type of change will need to be systemic, making changes in the entire infrastructure of schools as we know them. Schools will require a whole new conceptualization in many elements of infrastructure, including how we structure the subjects or courses, the age segregation through grade levels, and the ways in which we teach (Veen & Vrakking, 2006).

The imperative of having a learner-centered classroom goes beyond meeting the learning needs of individual students. A teacher's responsibility to educate always has had implications that go beyond the classroom based on the fact that educators prepare students to interact with the outside world. Dewey (1916) claimed, "Discipline, natural development, culture, social efficiency, are moral traits—marks of a person who is a worthy member of that society which it is the business of education to further" (p. 359). To aid students in their ethical contribution to knowledge is critical. Seemiller and Grace (2018) extend this application, stating:

> Instead of helping students explore only their interests and viable career options, educators may also need to help students engage in self-exploration of their values and passions as they search for their greater meaning in life. (p. 24)

In this statement, Seemiller and Grace (2018) acknowledge the importance of the student experience. As part of a learner-centered curriculum, teachers must consider diverse populations with a variety of interests and backgrounds when using forms of media in the classroom.

CONCLUSIONS

Future classroom instruction and curriculum will need to be personalized to the needs of the individual learner (Hines & Whittington, 2017). In addition to understanding individuals' strengths, weaknesses, deficits, and abilities, educators must take into account their pacing needs and how the trajectory, depth, and medium of an individual's knowledge consumption and application may be different than his peers. Customizing education for the individual learner will not be an easy task; arguably, it may be impossible in the current school settings. However, that does not negate the fact that it is what Gen Zers and future generations need. Gen Z students are future innovators and creators of new possibilities for future generations. Perhaps this indicates that the greatest contribution of educators is preparing this generation to use their incredibly powerful position in history for intentional social justice change, ethical communication, curiosity, and critical discernment of information.

REFERENCES

Abbas, J., & Agosto, D. E. (2013). Youth and online social networking: What do we know so far? In J. Beheshti & A. Large (Eds.), *The information behavior of a new generation: Children and teens in the 21st century* (pp. 65–92). Lanham, MD: Scarecrow Press.

An, Y., & Reigeluth, C. (2011). Creating technology-enhanced, learner-centered classrooms: K–12 teachers' beliefs, perceptions, barriers, and support needs. *Journal of Digital Learning in Teacher Education, 28*(2), 54–62.

Barnes, K., Marateo, R. C., & Pixy Ferris, S. (2007). Teaching and learning with the Net generation. *Innovate: Journal of Online Education, 3*(4). Retrieved from https://nsuworks.nova.edu/innovate/vol3/iss4/1.

Bauerlein, M. (2008). *The dumbest generation.* New York, NY: Jeremy P. Tarcher/Penguin.

Bell, M. A. (2011). Native knowledge: Knowing what they know—and learning how to teach the rest. In M. Manafy & H. Gautschi (Eds.), *Dancing with digital natives* (pp. 351–372). Medford, NJ: Information Today.

Bebell, D., & Kay, R. (2010). One to one computing: A summary of the quantitative results from the Berkshire Wireless Learning Initiative. *Journal of Technology, Learning, and Assessment, 9*(2). Retrieved from http://www.jtla.org.

Bebell, D., & O'Dwyer, L. M. (2010). Educational outcomes and research from 1:1 computing settings. *Journal of Technology, Learning and Assessment, 9*(1), 4–15.

Blocher, J. M., Armfield, S. W., Sujo-Montes, L., Tucker, G., & Willis, E. (2011). Contextually based professional development. *Computers in the Schools, 28*(2), 158–169.

Brown, J. S. (2000). Growing up digital: How the web changes work, education, and the ways people learn. *Change*, March/April, 10–20.

Collins, A., & Halverson, R. (2009). *Rethinking education in the age of technology: The digital revolution and schooling in America.* New York, NY: Teachers College Press.

Cuban, L. (1986). *Teachers and machines: The classroom use of technology since 1920.* New York, NY: Teachers College Press.

Cuban, L. (2001). *Oversold and underused: Computers in the classroom.* Cambridge, MA: Harvard University.

Dimock, M. (2018). Defining generations: Where millennials end and post-millennials begin. *Pew Research Center.* Retrieved from http://www.pewresearch.org/fact-tank/2018/03/01/defining-generations-where-millennials-end-and-post-millennials-begin/.

Dewey, J. (1916). *Democracy and education: An introduction to the philosophy of education.* New York, NY: The Free Press.

Ertmer, P. A., & Ottenbreit-Leftwich, A. T. (2010). Teacher technology change: How knowledge, confidence, beliefs, and culture intersect. *Journal of Research on Technology in Education, 42*(3), 255–284.

Gardner, H. (2010). Five minds for the future. In J. Bellanca & R. Brandt (Eds.), *21st Century skills: Rethinking how students learn* (pp. 9–31). Bloomington, IN: Solution Tree Press.

Glendinning, S. (2018). A new rootedness? Education in the technological age. *Studies in Philosophy Education, 37*, 81–96.

Hines, A., & Whittington, A. (2017). Nine emerging student needs. *On the Horizon, 25*(3), 181–189.

Kim, C., Kim, M. K., Lee, C., Spector, J. M., & Demeester, K. (2013). Teacher beliefs and technology integration. *Teaching and Teacher Education, 29*, 76–85.

Kirschner, P. A., & Bruyckere, P. D. (2017). The myths of the digital native and the multitasker. *Teaching and Teacher Education, 67*, 135–142.

Mayer, R. E. (2009). *Multi-media learning* (2nd ed.). Cambridge, UK: Cambridge University Press.

Mayer, R. E. (2005). Cognitive theory of multimedia learning. In R. E. Mayer (Ed.), *The Cambridge handbook of multimedia learning* (pp. 31–48). Cambridge, UK: Cambridge University Press.

Oblinger, D. G., & Oblinger, J. L. (2005). *Educating the net generation.* Boulder, CO: EDUCAUSE.

Palfrey, J., & Gasser, U. (2016). *Born digital: How children grow up in a digital age.* New York, NY: Basic Books.

Prenksy, M. (2001). Digital natives, digital immigrants. *On the Horizon, 9*(5), 1–6.

Rosen, L. D. (2007). *Me, MySpace, and I: Parenting the net generation.* New York, NY: Palgrave Macmillan.

Seemiller, C., & Grace, M. (2017). Generation Z: Educating and engaging the next generation of students. *About Campus*, July–August, 21–26. DOI: 10.1002/abc.21293

Smith, F. J. (1913, July 9). The evolution of the motion picture: Looking into the future with Thomas A. Edison. *New York Dramatic Mirror*, pp. 24, 42.

Tapscott, D. (1998). *Growing up digital: The rise of the net generation.* New York, NY: McGraw-Hill.

Tapscott, D. (1999). Educating the net generation. *Educational Leadership, 56*(5), 6–11.

Vatanartiran, S., & Karadeniz, S. (2015). A needs analysis for technology integration plan: Challenges and needs of teachers. *Contemporary Educational Technology, 6*(3), 206–220.

Veen, W., & Vrakking, B. (2006). *Homo zappiens: Growing up in the digital age.* London, UK: Network Continuum Education.

Chapter 6

Multimedia Learning for a New Generation of Educators

Charles Lowery

INTRODUCTION

The classroom of the past century has been one predominantly comprised of strict mono-media instruction: a single stream of input powered and controlled by the audio of one teacher's voice, supported only occasionally with visual scaffolding through the use of one-dimensional print on chalkboards or dry-erase boards and in unwieldy textbooks. Even the classroom design was formed with desks in rows to better facilitate the projection of the teacher's single-channel delivery from the front of the class. This same format continues in many classrooms today, while outside the classroom-world of the twentieth-century learning environment, the audiovisual universe of multimedia is constantly expanding—rapidly. As Baker (2010) posits,

> In the twenty-first century, "texts" and "literacy" are not limited to words on the page: they also apply to still and moving images, such as photographs, television, and film. Today, being literate also means understanding wikis, blogs, nings, digital media, and other new and emerging technologies. Unfortunately, many K–12 educators have yet to realize the benefits of teaching students with and about non-print media, what is today recognized as an important part of "media literacy." (p. 133)

Industrial-age mentalities are being outsourced by information-age modalities. And the information age is already giving way to a new digital age—a multimedia age of interaction and integration. Yet, by and large, educators have done very little to capitalize on the new possibilities available in this new age.

NEW GENERATION OF EDUCATORS

Researchers and practitioners in many fields—including education—see smart phones and tablets as toys and disregard their potential to be tools. However, as at least one philosopher of technology attests, "Human life is thoroughly mediated by technology. It is hard even to imagine a life that didn't involve at least some tools and devices" (Tripathi, 2006, p. 1).

New technologies have long mediated human interaction with the world. Consider the vehicle that conveys the majority of humanity to and from their jobs, across the grid of intricately designed streets to the building drafted by computer-aided architecture. Much like the manner in which television programs provide countless viewers their evening news and hours on hours of entertainment—and entertainment synonymous with learning channels such as History, Discovery, and PBS—technology and media are both catalysts and continuum for occupation. The educational potential of new devices cannot be discounted simply because of their handheld status and capacity to provide diversion. Innovations such as the earliest automobiles and first TV sets could easily have been called irrelevant diversions; however, innovative thinkers and entrepreneurs recognized ways to convert these passing fads into meaningful staples of people's lives and livelihoods.

Collins (2001) warns that technology should not be a creator of momentum, that "you cannot make good use of technology until you know which technologies are relevant" (pp. 152–153). That may be true for the corporate world, but perhaps the learning community should consider a different stance. At the moment, technology use in the classroom is quasi-relevant. The term *quasi-relevant* is used because it is relevant to the students' world, but its full capability as a learning media is still nascent. New generations of teachers will need to be the innovators of technology and multimedia as we progress farther into this century.

Similarly, in the introduction of Michael Fullan's *All Systems Go*, Senge (2010) acknowledges

> the growing gap between what [students] need to be able to understand (such as alternative cultures and social-technological-ecological systems) and to do (such as work collaboratively to solve complex interdependent problems) and what we have traditionally taught is the primary reason so many young people find school less and less relevant for their lives. (p. xi)

In this new era of career and college readiness, teachers dedicated to education will need to understand the potential role for multimedia learning in creating complex learning environments that foster relevance for digital learners. What is needed is a theoretical framework that grounds practicing teachers and teacher preparation programs in a deeper understanding of multimedia engagement, environment, and how integration of content and multimedia technology can enhance learner perception and lesson presentation.

TOWARD A NEW MULTIMEDIA LEARNING THEORY

Multimedia learning theory hinges on the concept that learners perceive the world through multiple senses—that is, audio and visual—what Mayer (2001), borrowing from Paivio (1986), calls *dual coding*. Mayer and Moreno (1998) expand on this to explain the cognitive processes in which the learner engages via multimedia learning, selecting, organizing, and integrating. To summarize, the learner perceives words and pictures that enter the sensory memory through the eyes and ears, the sounds and images are filtered, and then the relevant elements are selected to proceed for processing in the working memory; here, the information is organized into mental, verbal, and visual models, which are integrated and connected with the learner's prior knowledge to be stored in the student's long-term memory (Doolittle, 2002).

This fundamental description of how multimedia potentially can impact learning can be further reduced to this: information is perceived through audio and visual channels and processed as coherent and meaningful mental representations. As described, students always have learned using the "multimedia" model: students perceived the teacher's voice (audio) and/or print and pictures in a textbook (visual); the brain processed the input—as long as it was comprehensible—into coherent models in the students' short-term memory; then connections were made to background knowledge and internalized. However, for the student to link any new information to previous information, it must be relevant to the learner.

Whether a teacher views a student simply as a sensory learner—that is, an auditory, visual, or tactile learner—or as one of Gardner's (1983) "intelligences," matters not. All students (i.e., all human beings) perceive the world and build relevance through a multiple of natural (e.g., eyes) and synthetic (e.g., eyeglasses) media. Each medium can be viewed as a mode of learning—a method of perception—that appeals either to a perceiver's audio-visual-tactile-olfactory-gustatory input or to a learner's "mental powers . . . *rationality, intelligence*, or the deployment of *mind*" (Gardner, 1983, p. 5). By extension, this includes multimedia resources as a means of delivering and receiving information or instruction.

Arguably, advancing technologies have made the multimedia world *the* reality for all children in this generation. Teachers, now more than ever, will need to consider the multimedia world in which their students live and collaboratively work together with other educators to understand the relevance of that environment and apply it to the acquisition of new emerging knowledge.

Relevance seems both simple and obvious. Nevertheless, for learning to be relevant it must directly relate to the student through both learner perception and teacher presentation. Perception refers to the manner in which the student receives and makes meaning of information. A student's personal interest and intelligence style are components that affect the way in which the learner perceives and processes instruction. Presentation considers the methods and strategies teachers employ to design, differentiate, and deliver lessons.

Moreover, presentation encompasses the learning environment as the delineated realm in which the student interacts with the presented information, both prior to and in the act of processing. Therefore, presentation can extend to the student's means of exhibiting what has been learned—his or her presentation as a multimedia project or product.

To better frame the concept of perception, consideration must be given to interest and the role it plays. Students perceive best when interested in the subject. For more than a century educational philosophy has recognized the importance of student interest. Dewey (1903) recognizes a need to appeal to a child's senses,

> to direct eye and ear . . . to what is present before him in such a way as to impress those things upon memory, while at the same time getting his mental imagery free to work upon matters of real interest to him. (p. 10)

Further, Dewey expresses the importance of creating interest in teaching:

> Interest is first active, projective, or propulsive. We take interest. To be interested in any matter is to be actively concerned with it. The mere feeling regarding a subject may be static or inert but interest is dynamic . . . Wherever there is interest there is response in the way of feeling. (p. 13)

A dynamic response is the result of students being actively concerned, or to employ more contemporary terminology, time on task, active participation, or being engaged in the instruction or information as presented. In other words, a given student will perceive completely and fully only what interests that particular student.

The importance of interest has manifested in recent years as the anticipatory set or "hook," made popular by Hunter's (1982) lesson cycle for mastery teaching, and the "engage" phase, as presented in Bybee's (1997) 5E model of instruction. In the twenty-first century, students both perceive and have interest in the technological—in fact, students born after the commercialization of the internet in 1995 have been engaged with a technology-enhanced lifeworld since birth. The Public Education Visioning Institute (2012) thoughtfully recognizes that:

> In today's digital world, most students come to school computer and technology savvy. With their iPods, iPhones, computer games, social networking pages, and text messaging, they routinely use multimedia and Internet resources in their daily lives. Technology development has also resulted in widespread change in the way students learn. To keep students fully engaged, schools must adapt to this new and rapidly changing environment. They must embrace the potential of new technologies and make optimum use of the digital devices and connections that are prevalent today to make learning vibrant and stimulating for all. (p. 1)

More and more teachers are recognizing the way in which learning can become "vibrant and stimulating for all" through multimedia learning. Mrs. Thomas, an instructional strategist with thirteen years of teaching experience, acknowledges,

> Multimedia tools are useful in engaging the twenty-first-century learner. In this way, the teacher benefits because the students are more receptive to learn. As advances in technology are made, teachers should not be expected or expect to hold the attention of their class without incorporating these tools. Even young children are accustomed to interacting with technology whether it is a smartphone, nook/kindle, or home computer. How can educators expect them to abandon these during the eight-hour school day? If students are not engaged, how well are they learning the material? (S. Thomas, personal communication, February 19, 2012)

Mrs. Thomas's colleague, Mrs. Asbill, echoes her observations, stating that multimedia learning is "engaging . . . both intellectually and socially. Clearly, students learn when they are engaged. It creates both a purpose and enjoyment" (R. Asbill, personal communication, February 18, 2012).

Educators such as Mrs. Thomas and Mrs. Asbill recognize that students are completely vested and driven by all things digital. In fact, the technology-enhanced world in which they have developed is the very nature of *their* world—their usernames and avatars are as much a part of their identities and learning styles as Social Security cards and driver's licenses.

Contextualized in this world are their interests; they are a means of continuous engagement, diversion, and social and societal connection. To connect with the student requires teachers to connect within that space. In other words, the digital world has relevance to students as individuals and as social beings. Therefore, it follows that digital learners would view the technologically enriched multimedia modalities as the primary means of connecting with their generation's collective personality and the preferred lens through which to perceive the world.

The various and varied lifeworlds of today's learners exist in a common culture of technology. This digitalized culture has, in an analogous sense, hardwired and programmed our children for a technological interface. Accessing the digital environment potentially provides educators a much-needed platform to engage student interest, differentiate for heterogeneous demographics, and vary methodologies and modalities of brain-based learning. In this student-friendly world, students feel vested and validated. Many teachers and adults avoid this environment simply because they do not have an interest in it; students do.

In addition to perception, a benefit of multimedia learning is versatility of presentation. Access and availability for content permeate the Web and the world of the multimedia learner. Information is readily available at the click of a mouse; online banks of knowledge such as the Encyclopedia Britannica and the Education Resources Information Center (ERIC) update regularly; and countless videos covering any number of topics from how to play a favorite song on the piano to learning vocabulary in French, Spanish, or Navajo, from how to solve for variables to condensed, digestible summaries of heuristics and hermeneutics can be streamed from almost any electronic device.

These Web-based opportunities and the additional multimedia software products being developed offer teachers and students endless options in terms of accommodations, modifications, differentiated instruction, and multiple learning styles. Educators need to give much consideration to ways to filter, select, organize, and integrate this massive amount of attainable media into the learning environment in a purposeful and meaningful way.

Today's teachers must be mindful and careful of how they choose to disseminate or display this information. However, presentation does not end with display—it carries over into the learning activities of the students. Mrs. Tennison, an elementary reading coach with nineteen years as an educator, shares:

> Digital media is a very meaningful way for students to express their creativity, knowledge and problem-solving skills. Through platforms such as Glogster, Animoto, PowerPoint, and so many others, students can create projects by embedding text, sounds, photos, graphics, videos, drawings, data and more. Through [multimedia] learning, they learn content, but most importantly, they explore, and create a completely original masterpiece. These come to life when they share on the SMART boards and "teach" the class. (A. Tennison, personal communication, February 16, 2012)

The manner in which teachers allow students to interact with available resources—how they mine, manage, manipulate, discuss, reflect on, and critique the text and tones they encounter through multimedia learning—will be crucial to fostering digital literacy, criticality, communication skills, innovation, problem solving, and possibility.

If educators are going to make relationships and instruction relevant, they must cross the technology-enhanced boundary to a digital world with synchronous and asynchronous options. Methods of curriculum design and instructional delivery must consider a lifeworld couched in constantly emerging multimedia possibilities.

TEACHER PREPARATION PROGRAMS AND MULTIMEDIA

Elmore (2010) gives a rather conservative and, at times, dark view of the impact of technology on learning in our generation; however, he does admit, that

> Teachers must remember that a lecture isn't enough anymore—or at least we cannot *begin* with a lecture. If we want to be heard, we must engage [students'] interest with an experience that captures their imagination. They want to see something. They want action and interaction. (p. 49)

The author goes on to state that "adults—especially those of us who work as campus workers and teachers—cannot communicate [i.e., teach] the same way we did in the 1980s or even the 1990s and expect to be heard" (p. 51). Elmore's claim seems to be an understatement when considering the countless means and methods this century offers to differentiate and accommodate for current student learning preferences.

As more and more technologies surface, new potential and possibilities will need to be explored, developed, refined, and expanded. Interactive whiteboards, document cameras, digital presenters, data projectors, and other instructional technologies including virtual and haptic interfaces are constantly being developed, tweaked, and improved.

Needed are teachers with the courage to examine and integrate the theoretical and the practical aspects of multimedia into an engaging curriculum that will empower innovative learners who will be capable of critiquing and considering the possibilities of their native digital world. Teachers and educational leaders will need to stay abreast of and discriminate among a vast amount of research and technologies through collaboration and networking.

Teachers will need programs with courses designed to prepare them to appropriately select and use the vast array of multimedia devices and software. For example, Jacobs (2010) lists interactive whiteboards, webcams, laptop computers, e-mail accounts, iPods, and flip cameras as tools in teachers' "electronic backyard" (p. 25) to reconceptualize curriculum, enrich instruction, and upgrade assessments. As Jacobs puts it, "Just as Euripides and his fellow dramatists gave the world a new form with theater, new forms give us new platforms for thinking" (p. 27).

An understanding of Web-based media platforms such as Animoto, Glogster, Prezi, Preezo, SlideShare, Voicethread, Vuvox, Xtranormal, YouTube, Zentation, and numerous other Web 2.0 offerings, integrate motion, graphics, voice-overs, interaction, video, and text/print to synthesize lessons and learning opportunities with flow and dimension as well as flexibility and design. Ability to use the cloud through Google Docs (and other Google apps), DropBox, Evernote, iWork, Wikispaces, Wifitti, webinars, and social networks (including Facebook and Edumodo) as collaborative spaces within synchronous and asynchronous environments for digitally sharing ideas, co-editing, and developing projects not only for students but for fellow teachers can create a global community for lifelong learning and creativity.

Apple products and other tablets have numerous education apps that offer alternate techniques and a potential paradigm shift in the way basic information in science, math, history, spelling, vocabulary development, and reference skills are scaffolded, reviewed, and reinforced.

In addition to the Web-based media and handheld applications mentioned above, computer software such as MovieMaker, PhotoStory, and TumbleCloud provides students varied and diverse means to record, share, and show learning that allows authentic audiovisual experience and expression. November (2011) relates ways teachers can use screencasting, podcasting, blogging, wikispaces, video, and audio/video conferencing to create multimedia environments in which students can take on engaging and contributing roles, including researcher, collaboration coordinator, and curriculum reviewer.

The twenty-first-century educator will not only have to create and implement meaningful lesson plans and flipped lectures that include these elements, but also should learn to see herself as designer and innovator of relevant curriculum and authentic assessments that challenge and engage. Project-based learning theory, problem-based inquiry, constructivist methodologies, and developments in cognitive psychology will have a definite impact on multimedia software and instructional programs. In addition to fostering familiarity with interactive and touch devices such as interactive whiteboards, tablets, document cameras, digital cameras and smartphones, and other handheld devices, preparation programs will allow teachers to engage, explore, and evaluate existing and forthcoming technologically enhanced methods.

Along this same line, teacher preparation programs will need to advance theory and practice in areas of multiple intelligences, differentiation, and brain-based learning. Further, the current generation of educators will need to look at media marketers and costly commercialized programs such as Lexia, Scientific Learning, BrainPop, and EduSmart with a critical eye and evaluate the learning benefits against the financial commitment. By doing so, educators can develop into professionals adept at engaging every child, presenting multimedia information and imagery, and teaching essential knowledge and skills in an interactive and meaningful manner.

FROM DIGITAL CONSUMERS TO DYNAMIC PRODUCERS

Another aspect of the multimedia world of which teachers need to be cognizant is that it can quickly become a world of consumerism without expectation of contribution. Young people are being brought up to be strictly consumers of technology, not producers. For far too many students today, technology is merely a series of gratuitous images on the screen, the sole source entertainment venue of our era.

In many instances, commonplace technologies—movies, videos, gaming, audio books, and texting—serve as a means of disengagement. Many individuals, young and old, blindly use the availability of home-based and handheld devices to escape face-to-face interaction. It is easier to text someone a truncated message, never expect a reply, and never commit to an exchange of dialogue.

Teachers need to create opportunities for students to question why things are and how they got that way. Students today have ambitions to grow up and work for companies such as Google or Facebook, but, for the most part, they are never given genuine opportunities to engage in rich and rigorous discussions about operating systems, development of software, programming languages, and coding proficiency.

To use YouTube as a platform to present a student-generated documentary is one thing, but to have students consider what it means to generate their own platform like YouTube is quite another. Although on the surface this may seem irrelevant to multimedia learning theory, by providing students relevant interaction and experiences with media along with exercising the human ability to connect with one another, make meaning, and think critically about the world, teachers can legitimate the curiosity and creativity of the entire spectrum of students they serve.

The nuances of this interaction and legitimation find metaphor in the configuring of software, photography and cinematography, manipulation of color, editing principles, design of graphics and animation, functionality, conservation of memory, and integrity of image—all fundamental to multimedia in everyday situations.

The issue here is one of choice and hope. Not every student aspires to dedicate her life to the design, usability, and marketing of major internet search engines such as Google or Bing; not every student desires to become an entrepreneur like Facebook's Mark Zuckerberg or Twitter's Evan Williams; neither does every student aspire to go to college. As educators, the responsibility is to prepare them to have the option. Such preparation requires that students engage in relevant relationships with their mentors, teachers, role models, and fellow students—those in the seat next to them and those on another continent.

The field of education must seek out and develop professionals who are willing to present students with information, software, hardware, and an engaging multimedia learning environment and allow them to perceive the world at large, through history, current events, hands-on projects, interdisciplinary content, and multicultural contexts. A well-known website for educators, Edutopia (Simpson, 2008; Ellis, 2003, 2008; Curtis, 2003), offers several examples of how just such professionals can dynamically impact student learning through multimedia methods. Two are the Ferryway Magnet School in Malden, Massachusetts, and the Moanalua High School in Honolulu, Hawaii.

THE SAUGUS IRON WORKS PROJECT: FERRYWAY SCHOOL

The George Lucas Educational Foundation's Edutopia produces a plethora of blogs, guides, videos, and accompanying articles about exemplar schools that push meaningful instruction through multimedia methods. Among the numerous innovative schools heralded on this website, the Ferryway School offers an interesting consideration for multimedia learning theory.

The video blog titled "Using Today's Technology Tools to Study Yesterday's" (Ellis, 2008) showcases fifth graders from Malden in the Boston area on a field trip to the Saugus Iron Works, a national historic site. The video demonstrates how schools can engage multimedia learners, integrate state standards, and inspire students to become not only consumers of technology but producers as well. The visit to the historic mill is the culmination of a six-week unit designed to introduce students to state standards in science, history, and literacy through hands-on tasks, concept maps, choice, and internet research. At the site, students use digital cameras and "the latest technology tools to study the country's early innovations" (Ellis, 2008).

School technology specialist Robert Simpson supported teachers in the design of the project and helped to integrate technology in a purposeful way. In Simpson's (2008) words, "Teachers have done all the really good research and constructed the structure of how the students are going to navigate through that unit and ultimately what that does is it empowers the students to make decisions" (Ellis, 2008).

Simpson (2008) also provided the supplemental article on the Edutopia website. In the article, Simpson states that this project was "a new approach" teachers used to connect standards in science and history, areas in which students had performed poorly on state assessments. Simpson's online article provides links to the Ferryway School homepage; the National Park Service's Web page about Saugus Iron Works; "The Saugus Iron Works Great Adventure" website, which provides parents and teachers information about the project-based learning experience; and a link to a PDF of the concept map that lays out the way technology, instruction, analysis, and development were grounded in the curriculum.

The Saugus experience provides educators in the digital era with a practical, multidimensional model of multimedia learning. The video and article are intended to document the multimedia learning experience of a class of fifth graders in Massachusetts and show how the curriculum can be brought to life through such an endeavor. However, the final product as Edutopia presents it is more than just an example of what teachers can do. It demonstrates some specific advantages to such teaching.

First, it captures the experience as a learner-created artifact of future learning future generations. Although the project-based unit is perpetually accessible to anyone interested, the development and the design of the activity become the metaphor for multimedia possibilities. The example is one of perception and presentation, and engages not just the school-based learner alone, but the school-based learner becomes scientist, historian, journalist, and ultimately teacher for the entire global community. This is accentuated in the way that Edutopia serves as a platform—a digital museum of sorts—to exhibit the incorporation of text and photos of the article with the sounds, voices, and images in the video to immerse the viewer in a single multimedia event.

The second advantage to the project is simply how it demonstrates the potential of multimedia learning. Images, text, interviews, sounds, voices, all come together to form a meaningful multidimensional product.

Finally, the story illustrates how students are being introduced to the concept that technology is not only progressive but is progressing. Interest in the way things work and why those things work that way are present in this learning activity. In a powerful way, the Ferryway School project represents how students can use the multimedia lens to look at relics and artifacts from the past and contextualize their meaning and impact on their current life.

By doing so, students begin to think critically and proleptically about the way the actions and innovations of their generation will influence and modify the future. The Saugus Iron Works experiment, the collaborative spirit of the teachers, and the interest and engagement of the students create an environment in which students can question how things improve and how society moves forward.

DESIGN, DOCUMENTARY, AND DRAMA: MOANALUA HIGH SCHOOL

Students from Moanalua High School in Honolulu offer the way to express the meaning they construct in their lifeworlds through multimedia. They create documentaries questioning grading policies; engage in multimedia projects that integrate English and social studies, and design, film, edit, and give voice through narration to assignments on major world issues such as child labor and immigration.

One student filming a documentary regarding ESL students expresses the autobiographical value of the project, recognizing that her subject of choice "really hits close to home . . . Everybody in Hawaii has an immigrant background. We all came from somewhere else but unfortunately, even if we all are immigrants in a sense, we still discriminate against others" (Ellis, 2003). Moreover, according to teacher Lynne Sueoka,

> [Students applied] understandings that had come from *To Kill a Mockingbird*, that had come from civics, and the strong emotional reaction to *Of Mice and Men*, trying to think about in their own world instances of justice and injustice. And the whole goal of this is to seek truth through the video journalism, and then achieve justice. (Ellis, 2003)

By integrating language, the social sciences, and multimedia, teachers synthesize learning environments that include choice and variety, inspire student ownership, and give consideration to learning styles.

The project started as an experiment by Dan Hale, the drama teacher and Learning Center coordinator, who discovered that multimedia projects help to motivate his students, provoke them to participate, and excite them to ask questions—all signs of their interest and engagement. In the companion article (Curtis, 2003), Hale acknowledges that the program not only has an influence on the students' level of involvement, but directly impacts them academically as well: "All of sudden their achievement started going way up and they got real interested in the class" (p. 1).

The media integration experiment has evolved into a program that allows students to incorporate available multimedia resources to create oral histories, produce video self-portraits relating to metaphor, learn and engage in Japanese, and hold online international dialogues with students in Japan about perspectives on current issues and historical events including the bombing of Pearl Harbor. During their time in the program, students not only produce documentaries and Web pages, but also integrate literature, lighting, voice, and multimedia knowledge to stage dramas and direct short films.

As Hale comments, for students, "it's not just a matter of doing a bunch of papers, getting a grade back, and walking on. They're actually doing something that's bringing together a lot of different things and they do take pride in it" (Ellis, 2003).

Teachers in the program value the technology as a means of providing an element of criticality to the academics and core curriculum (Curtis, 2003). According to Sueoka, the way in which the lessons are designed, taking into account student personality and diverse learners, "forces students to communicate in a different way—a way that requires them to really know the material" (Curtis, 2003, p. 1). Communication as critical thinking is expressed through voice-overs, video clips, and provocative background music in ethnographical and literary multimedia projects that address equity, social justice, and cultural diversity.

The work being accomplished at Moanalua High School, by both teachers and students, demonstrates the basic potential of multimedia to empower every individual and give voice to all stakeholders. Students are learning just how relevant the core curriculum can be to their lives. Teachers and leaders in schools such as Moanalua have keyed in on the idea that technology has the potential to be the textbook, the blackboard, *and* the pen and paper of last century.

They recognize the value of using available technologies as a means of motivating their children by engaging them in an environment that is relevant to their lifeworld. Just as these technologies from our history were employed to provide access to a curriculum based on an agrarian and industrialized world, the new technologies—multimedia and more—provide learners an entry into an ever-changing, information-driven, digitalized society.

PDA—POWER-DOWN ACTIVITIES

No discussion of multimedia learning is complete without consideration of the downside of not powering down. November (2011) exhorts, "If we do not teach students social responsibility and ethics, then our worst fears of children abusing these tools will come true" (p. 3). Teachers of the twenty-first century must not allow their learners to get lost in the virtual labyrinth of cyber offerings. Ceaseless connection to others through multimedia channels potentially has a dehumanizing and image-altering effect on students' relationships and development of social interaction.

Canadian educator and phenomenologist Max van Manen (2010) builds on the metaphor of Momus, the Greek god of sarcasm, satire, and secrecy (or privacy), to explore the negative and addictive impact that "computer-mediated social networks as well as the modes of contact afforded by mobile technologies" can have—not only on students and children, but on users of all ages (p. 3). For van Manen, "Contemporary Momus technologies allow people to feel close and in touch while they may be separated in space in time" (p. 3).

The influence that social networking and multimedia interactions have on the identities of individuals and their understanding of human intimacy and personal privacy is an issue that educators need to keep in mind. Pseudo-identities via faux social media accounts and avatars potentially can distort a student's self-image and understanding of authentic human interface.

Nevertheless, technologies have been criticized from this angle for centuries. Progress of any sort when not critically examined and properly employed can produce ill-conceived outcomes—from the first flash of fire to the harnessing of electricity. Educators will need to be cognizant of the negative impact while focusing students on the positive effects. In a sense, educators will need to know how to "beat swords into plowshares, and spears into pruning hooks," as it is said in the book of Isaiah 2:4. For centuries, stonemasons have understood how to properly form then wield the trowel, compass, and square to create the intricate cathedrals and temples of the ages; likewise, teachers will need to form a multimedia curriculum and use available and nascent technologies with professional concern and personal compassion.

The multimedia lifeworld of today's students exists both pre- and post-classroom as well as concurrently with it. Teachers in the twenty-first century will need to validate these students to reach them where they are.

Employing technology-enhanced modalities, whether with Facebook or FaceTime, does not mean that humanity has to be pushed aside or undermined. It does not presuppose a world in which students cannot be taught the value of powering down and engaging in real face-to-face intimacy and authentic social interaction. Now, more than ever, educators need to provide authentic (and aesthetic) environments in which students can define their individuality/identity and simultaneously interact with other human beings socially and sincerely.

CONCLUSION

Van Manen (2010) asks how educators, in the context of present-day Momus technologies, can create meaningful lived experiences for studies in the midst of the privatization of the public and the publicization of the private. However, educators need to know that Momus was not only the god of critical judgment but was also the god of authors and poets. Criticality and creativity most often go hand in hand. This is a vital part of twenty-first-century curriculum design and the development of learning experiences using multimedia technologies. Planning, brainstorming, discussing, designing, reflecting, and other independent and cooperative activities easily can be developed to accentuate all learning opportunities.

Ferryway's Saugus Iron Works project and Moanalua High's dramatic performances and student-driven projects demonstrate that this can be accomplished prior to, as a part of, and after multimedia projects being implemented and make the multimedia learning even more meaningful. These types of assignments can guide students into humbling and humanizing searches of the global world at large as well as efforts to bring about social justice and democracy in their own backyards.

Most important, teachers do not have to be the omniscient erudite of all things technological. Although they should, as encouraged here, possess an understanding and be willing to research possible multimedia methodologies, educators must be able to validate the knowledge of the student. When teachers dare to learn from their students, students come to see their lives and background knowledge as genuinely validated. Teachers must know how teaching the students can also mean learning from the students. In this manner, the learning environment can develop collectively and collaboratively, and can evolve as multimedia opportunities are likewise evolving, exponentially.

The concepts regarding multimedia as expressed here have assumed that practitioners understand that the learning theory has evolved from Mayer's (2001) dual channels of audiovisual processing into a dynamic network of teaching tools, social networks, and learning platforms. Practicing teachers in the new multimedia generation will need to become informed risk takers, innovators, and educated researchers who integrate, experiment, and investigate the multimedia "tools and toys," as well as the association of software and hardware to excite the curiosity, creativity, and criticality of the children in their classrooms and then allow them access to the audiovisual world of information, animation, and virtual learning at their fingertips.

REFERENCES

Baker, F. W. (2010). Media literacy: 21st century literacy skills. In H. H. Jacobs (Ed.), *Curriculum 21: Essential education for a changing world.* Alexandria, VA: ASCD.

Bybee, R. W. (1997). *Achieving scientific literacy: From purpose to practices.* Portsmouth, NH: Heinemann.

Collins, J. (2001). *Good to great.* New York, NY: Collins.

Curtis, D. (2003, August 5). Multimedia motivation: Helping kids love to learn. Retrieved from http://edutopia.org/.

Dewey, J. (1903). *Interest as related to will.* Chicago, IL: University of Chicago Press.

Doolittle, P. E. (2002). *Multimedia learning: Empirical results and practical applications.* Retrieved from http://scr.csc.noctrl.edu.

Ellis, K. (Producer). (2003, August 5). Integrated studies in Honolulu: Moanalua High School [video file]. Retrieved from http://www.edutopia.org/.

Ellis, K. (Producer). (2008, June 25). Using today's technology tools to study yesterday's [video file]. Retrieved from http://www.edutopia.org.

Elmore, T. (2010). *Generation iY: Our last chance to save their future.* Atlanta, GA: Poet Gardener Publishing.

Fullan, M. (with Senge, P.). (2010). *All systems go: The change imperative for whole system reform.* Thousand Oaks, CA: Corwin Press.

Gardner, H. E. (1983). *Frames of mind: The theory of multiple intelligences.* New York, NY: Basic Books.

Hunter, M. (1982). *Mastery teaching.* Thousand Oaks, CA: Corwin Press.

Jacobs, H. H. (2010). Upgrading the curriculum: 21st century assessment types and skills. In H. H. Jacobs (Ed.), *Curriculum 21: Essential education for a changing world.* Alexandria, VA: ASCD.

Mayer, R. E. (2001). *Multimedia learning.* Cambridge, UK: Cambridge University Press.

Mayer, R. E., & Moreno, R. (1998). *A cognitive theory of multimedia learning: Implications for design principles.* Retrieved from http://esoluk.co.uk/calling/pdf/chi.pdf.

November, A. (2011). Students as contributors: The digital learning farm. *Instructional Leader, 24*(5), 1–3.

Paivio, A. (1986). *Mental representations: A dual coding approach.* Oxford, UK: Oxford University Press.

Public Education Visioning Institute. (2012). Creating a new vision for public education in Texas. *Instructional Leader, 25*(2), 1–8.

Simpson, R. (2008, June 25). Visualizing technology integration: A model for meeting ISTE educational-technology standards. Retrieved from http://edutopia.org.

Tripathi, A. K. (2006). *Culture of embodiment and technology reflection.* Professor D. Ihde's technoscience research seminar. Stony Brook University, October 2006.

Van Manen, M. (2010). The pedagogy of Momus technologies: Facebook, privacy, and online intimacy. *Qualitative Health Research, 20*(10), 1–10.

Chapter 7

What Do Teachers and Administrators Need to Know about Multimedia Learning Theory?

Richard E. Mayer

INTRODUCTION

Suppose you were asked to read a textbook chapter on the history of distance education that contained printed words and illustrations, view a narrated animation explaining how ocean waves work, play an interactive educational game containing on-screen explanations and graphics intended to teach how electrical circuits work, or attend a slideshow presentation using illustrations and text on how a virus causes a cold. In each case you would be engaged in multimedia learning, which is defined as learning from words and pictures (Mayer, 2009). In multimedia learning, the words may be printed or spoken, and the pictures may be static (such as illustrations or photos) or dynamic (such as animation or video).

Multimedia instruction occurs when students receive both words and pictures that are intended to promote learning, including illustrated textbooks, computer-based narrated animations, interactive computer games containing on-screen words and graphics, and face-to-face slideshow presentations. Multimedia instruction can be delivered with media ranging from books, to computers, to face-to-face venues. This chapter will examine what teachers and administrators need to know about multimedia learning.

WHY IS MULTIMEDIA LEARNING IMPORTANT FOR EDUCATION?

As a teacher or administrator, you are called upon to play the roles of creator and consumer of multimedia instruction. When you prepare a PowerPoint slideshow or a printed document intended for teaching, for example, you become a creator of multimedia instruction. When you select a textbook or educational software intended for teaching, you become a consumer of multimedia instruction. The goal of this chapter is help the reader become a more effective creator and consumer of multimedia instruction by introducing you to a research-based theory of how people form words and graphics and by summarizing research-based principles for how to design effective multimedia instruction.

For hundreds of years, the primary vehicle for instruction has been words, including oral presentations and printed textbooks. More recently, advances in computer technology have enabled the creation of breathtaking graphics, including animation, video, illustrations, and photos that can be easily created and delivered to learners.

An important research question for educators concerns whether there is any benefit when graphics are added to text, which is a form of what I call *value-added research*. For the past twenty years, my colleagues and I at the University of California, Santa Barbara, have conducted more than one hundred experiments on how to design multimedia instruction in ways that enable learners to take what they have learned and use it to solve problems in new situations (Mayer, 2009).

This focus on the effects of past learning on new learning is the classic issue of transfer, which has a long history both in psychology and education, dating back to the early days of both fields. In this chapter, I share an example of up-to-date research on teaching for transfer that may be relevant for teachers and administrators, by sharing some of the fruits of our research program on multimedia learning as well as other research from around the world on what works with multimedia instruction (Mayer, 2005a; O'Neil, 2005).

WHAT IS THE MULTIMEDIA PRINCIPLE?

Consider the following description of how a bicycle tire pump works, taken from a larger encyclopedia entry that also contained a description of the pump:

> As the rod is pulled out, air passes through the piston and fills the area between the piston and the outlet valve. As the rod is pushed in, the inlet valve closes and the piston forces air through the outlet value.

As you can see, this description uses words only and can be considered our control condition (i.e., words alone). In taking a value-added approach, we can ask whether students would learn more deeply if we added appropriate graphics to the text. For example, figure 7.1 contains a frame showing the state of the pump when the handle is up and a frame showing the state of

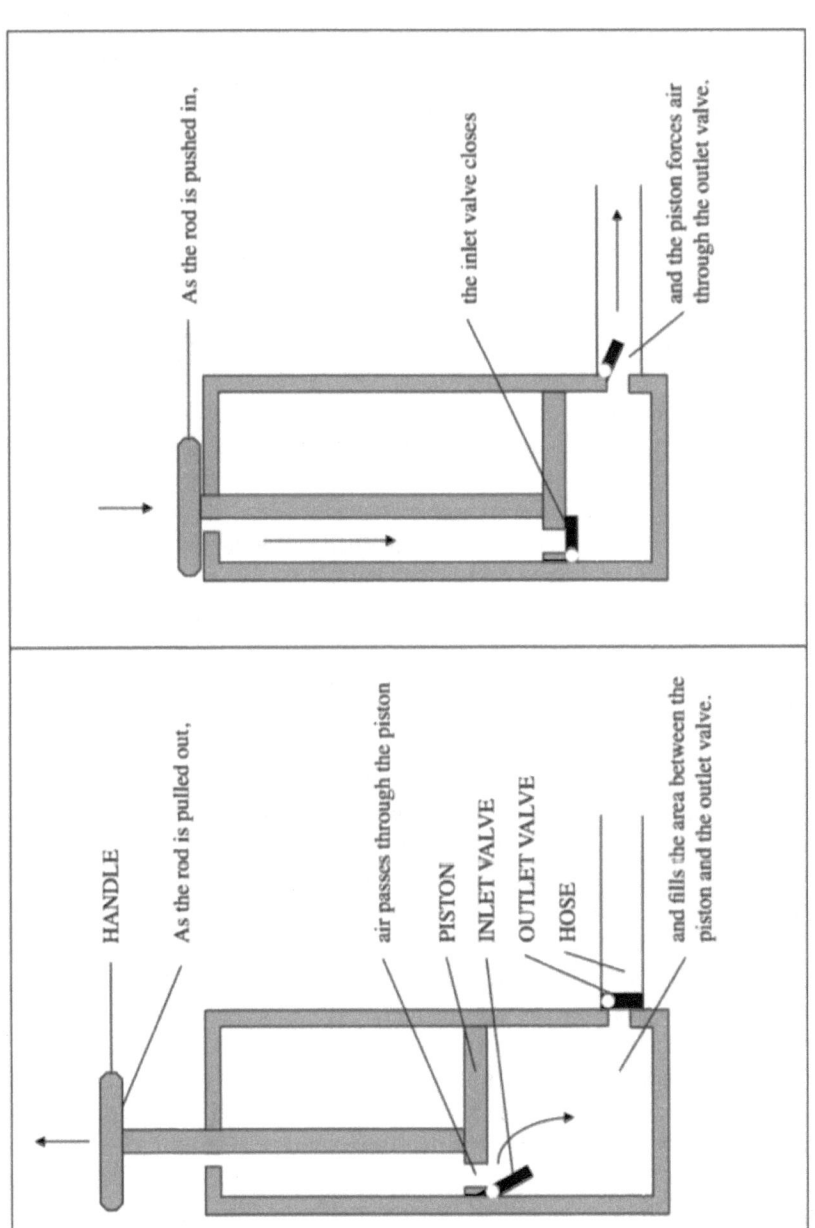

Figure 7.1.

the pump when the handle is down, using the exact same words as in the encyclopedia text. This set of annotated frames constitutes our experimental condition (i.e., words and pictures).

In order to conduct a value-added study, we could compare the learning outcomes of students who receive words only versus the learning outcomes of students who receive words and pictures. In this way, we can detect the value of adding graphics to text. To measure learning outcomes, we can include retention items (which gauge how much people remember) such as, "Please write down how a bicycle tire pump works."

In addition, we can include transfer items (intended to gauge how well people can use what they have learned in new situations) such as, "Suppose you pull up and push down on the handle of the pump several times but no air comes out. What could have gone wrong?" or "What could be done to make a pump more effective, that is, to move more air more rapidly?"

When we asked students to read the text-only lesson and then answer some retention and transfer questions, they did not perform very well (Mayer & Gallini, 1990). However, when we asked students to read the text-and-pictures lesson, they performed much better on answering retention and transfer questions. To compute the effect size (called Cohen's "d"), we subtracted the mean score of the control group (text only) from the mean score of the experimental group (text and pictures) and divided by the pooled standard deviation of the two groups. For both retention and transfer, the effect size was greater than $d = 1.00$, which means that the experimental group performed one standard deviation better than the control group.

We obtained similar results with effect sizes greater than $d = 1.00$ when we compared students who learned about pumps from a narrated animation, as summarized in figure 7.2, versus narration only (Mayer & Anderson, 1991). I am most interested in instructional features that improve transfer performance, so in the rest of this chapter I focus only on effect sizes for transfer.

Effect size is a particularly useful metric for teachers and administrators who are interested in instructional effectiveness because it provides an indication of the practical value of an instructional intervention (such as adding graphics). Effect size is particularly appropriate for value-added research, in which we compare the learning outcomes (as measured by a transfer test) of students who learned with a base version of a lesson versus an enhanced version that contains one additional instructional feature.

Cohen (1988) suggests that an effect size of $d = 0.20$ is small, $d = 0.50$ is medium, and $d = 0.80$ is large. An effect size of $d = 0.40$ or greater is generally considered important for education (Hattie, 2009). In this chapter, I focus on instructional features in multimedia instruction that create effect sizes of at least $d = 0.40$ on transfer tests.

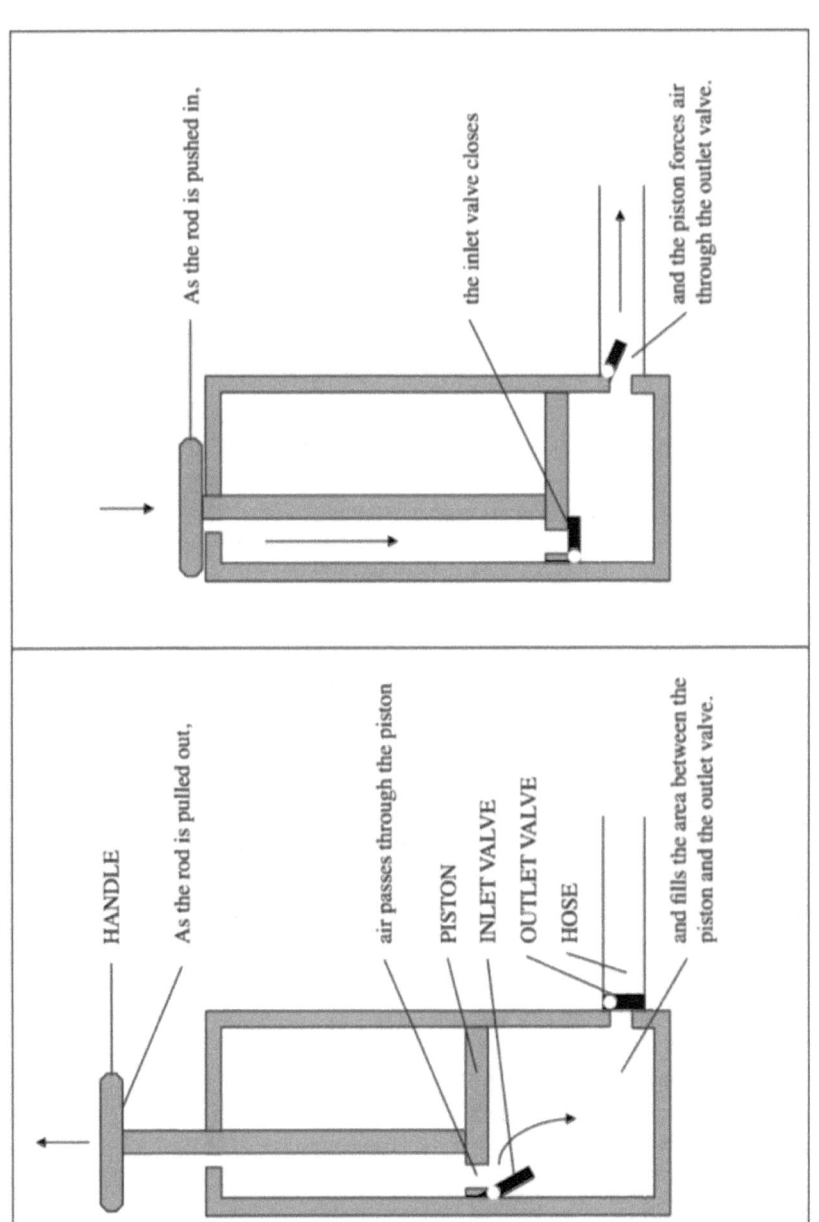

Figure 7.1.

the pump when the handle is down, using the exact same words as in the encyclopedia text. This set of annotated frames constitutes our experimental condition (i.e., words and pictures).

In order to conduct a value-added study, we could compare the learning outcomes of students who receive words only versus the learning outcomes of students who receive words and pictures. In this way, we can detect the value of adding graphics to text. To measure learning outcomes, we can include retention items (which gauge how much people remember) such as, "Please write down how a bicycle tire pump works."

In addition, we can include transfer items (intended to gauge how well people can use what they have learned in new situations) such as, "Suppose you pull up and push down on the handle of the pump several times but no air comes out. What could have gone wrong?" or "What could be done to make a pump more effective, that is, to move more air more rapidly?"

When we asked students to read the text-only lesson and then answer some retention and transfer questions, they did not perform very well (Mayer & Gallini, 1990). However, when we asked students to read the text-and-pictures lesson, they performed much better on answering retention and transfer questions. To compute the effect size (called Cohen's "d"), we subtracted the mean score of the control group (text only) from the mean score of the experimental group (text and pictures) and divided by the pooled standard deviation of the two groups. For both retention and transfer, the effect size was greater than $d = 1.00$, which means that the experimental group performed one standard deviation better than the control group.

We obtained similar results with effect sizes greater than $d = 1.00$ when we compared students who learned about pumps from a narrated animation, as summarized in figure 7.2, versus narration only (Mayer & Anderson, 1991). I am most interested in instructional features that improve transfer performance, so in the rest of this chapter I focus only on effect sizes for transfer.

Effect size is a particularly useful metric for teachers and administrators who are interested in instructional effectiveness because it provides an indication of the practical value of an instructional intervention (such as adding graphics). Effect size is particularly appropriate for value-added research, in which we compare the learning outcomes (as measured by a transfer test) of students who learned with a base version of a lesson versus an enhanced version that contains one additional instructional feature.

Cohen (1988) suggests that an effect size of $d = 0.20$ is small, $d = 0.50$ is medium, and $d = 0.80$ is large. An effect size of $d = 0.40$ or greater is generally considered important for education (Hattie, 2009). In this chapter, I focus on instructional features in multimedia instruction that create effect sizes of at least $d = 0.40$ on transfer tests.

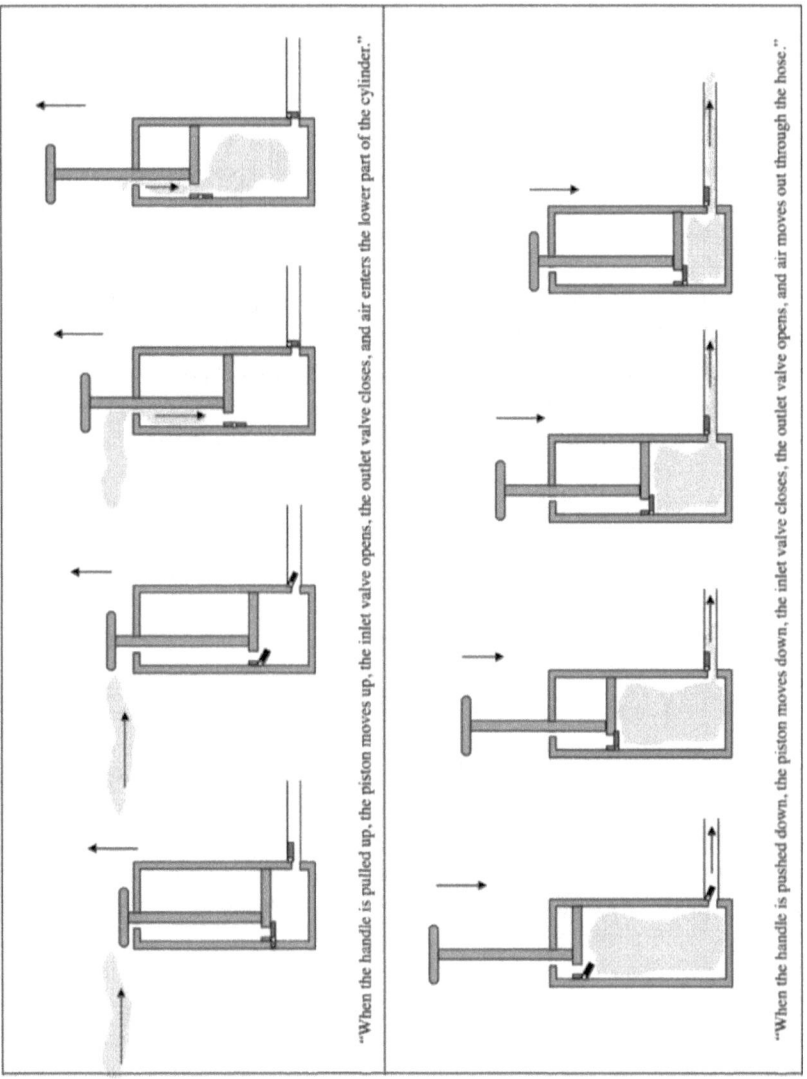

Figure 7.2.

People learn better from words and pictures than from words alone. This is a statement of the *multimedia principle*. Support for the multimedia principle comes from eleven experimental comparisons conducted in our lab.

Studies included paper-based lessons comparing printed text versus printed text and illustrations on brakes (Mayer, 1989, Experiments 1 and 2; Mayer & Gallini, 1990, Experiment 1), pumps (Mayer & Gallini, 1990, Experiment 2), electrical generators (Mayer & Gallini, 1990, Experiment 3), and lightning (Mayer, Bove, Bryman, Mars, & Tapangco, 1996, Experiment 2). Studies also included computer-based lessons comparing narration versus narration and animation on pumps (Mayer & Anderson, 1991, Experiment 2; Mayer & Anderson, 1991, Experiment 1), brakes (Mayer & Anderson, 1992, Experiment 2), lightning (Moreno & Mayer, 2002b, Experiment 1), and arithmetic (Moreno & Mayer, 1999a, Experiment 1). The median effect size favoring adding graphics to words is $d = 1.39$, which is a large effect.

The multimedia effect also has been found by numerous other researchers (Fletcher & Tobias, 2005). In short, the reason that teachers and administers might be interested in multimedia instruction is that it has been shown to be much more effective in promoting deep learning than instruction based solely on words. However, not all forms of multimedia instruction are equally effective, and it is quite easy to add graphics that do not improve learning or actually detract from it. Therefore, in the remainder of this chapter, I provide a theoretical framework for multimedia learning and a set of research-based principles for how to design effective multimedia instruction.

HOW DOES MULTIMEDIA LEARNING WORK?

Figure 7.3 provides a framework for explaining how multimedia works (Mayer, 2009). The boxes represent three memory stores in the learner's information processing system: *sensory memory*, which briefly holds what comes in through the learner's eyes as a visual image and what comes in through the learner's ears as an auditory sound; *working memory*, which can temporarily hold and manipulate a few sounds and images; and *long-term memory*, which is the learner's permanent storehouse of knowledge.

The arrows represent three basic cognitive processes in the learner's information processing system—selecting incoming images and sounds for further processing in working memory, organizing the images into a coherent pictorial representation and organizing the sounds into a coherent verbal representation in working memory; and integrating the pictorial and verbal representations with each other and with relevant knowledge activated from long-term memory. The model of the learner's information processing system shown in figure 7.3 is based on three principles derived from research

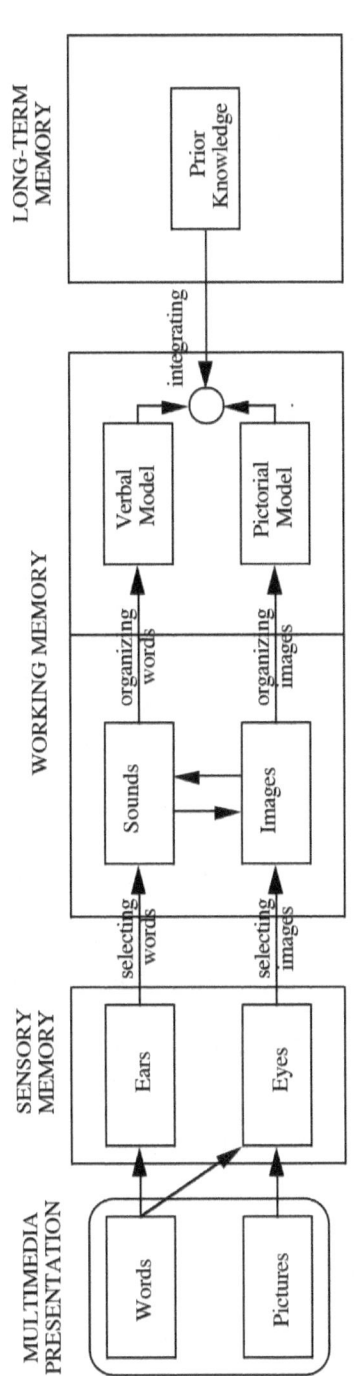

Figure 7.3.

in cognitive science—the *dual channels principle*, the *limited capacity principle*, and the *active processing principle*.

The dual channels principle states that people have separate channels for processing visual and verbal information (Paivio, 1986, 2007), as indicated by the two parallel rows in figure 7.3 (with the verbal channel on the top and the visual channel on the bottom). The limited capacity principle states that people can process only a few items in each channel in working memory at any one time (Baddeley, 1999), as indicated in the *working memory* box.

The active processing principle states that meaningful learning occurs when people engage in appropriate cognitive processing during learning (Mayer, 2009; Wittrock, 1989), including selecting incoming information for further processing, mentally organizing the selected material into a coherent representation, and integrating visual and verbal representations with each other and with relevant knowledge activated from long-term memory, as indicated by the arrows in figure 7.3. Although learners must engage in all of the processing needed for meaningful learning, they are constrained by having to work within an information processing system that has limited capacity.

Consider what happens in your information processing system shown in figure 7.3 when you are given a multimedia lesson, such as a narrated animation describing how a pump works (indicated in the leftmost part of the figure). The spoken words enter your auditory sensory memory through your ears, and the graphics enter your visual sensory memory through your eyes, where they remain for only a fraction of a second before fading away. If you pay attention (indicated by the *selecting words* and *selecting pictures* arrows), some of the information is transferred to working memory for further processing (indicated as *sounds* and *images* in the left side of *working memory*).

In working memory, if you mentally organize the incoming words (indicated by the *organizing words* arrow), you can form a verbal model (indicated in the right side of *working memory*); and if you mentally organize the incoming images (indicated by the *organizing images* arrow), you can form a pictorial mental model (indicated in the right side of *working memory*). Finally, you can make connections between the verbal and pictorial models, and you can activate relevant prior knowledge from your storehouse in long-term memory and bring it into working memory so you can integrate it with incoming information (as indicated by the *integrating* arrow).

HOW DOES MULTIMEDIA INSTRUCTION WORK?

As you can see, learning depends on the learner engaging in appropriate processing during learning—including selecting, organizing, and integrating (Mayer, 2011a, 2011b). Thus, the goal of instruction is to present the to-be-learned material and to help guide the learner's cognitive processing during learning. However, the challenge facing instructional designers is that the limited capacity of working memory will allow for only a limited amount of processing within each channel at any one time.

Suppose you are asked to read a textbook explanation of the Doppler effect, for which the text says, "See figure 2," but you have to turn the page to see the figure. This is an example of what I call *extraneous processing* because you have to engage in wasted scanning back and forth between pages, resulting in a form of cognitive processing that does not help you learn about the Doppler effect.

Next, suppose you are asked to view a fast-paced narrated animation describing sixteen steps in lightning formation and containing a dozen new concepts (such as "positively charged particle" and "freezing level") that you are not sure you know. This creates what I call *essential processing* because you have to try to mentally represent a complicated cause-and-effect system in your mind as you watch the lesson. Finally, suppose I ask you to pause periodically and explain aloud each step in lightning formation as you view the narrated animation. This is an example of *generative processing*, in which you try to make sense of the presented material by reorganizing it and relating it to your prior knowledge.

Table 1 lists three demands on the learner's cognitive capacity during learning: *extraneous processing, essential processing,* and *generative processing* (Mayer, 2011a, 2011b; Sweller, 1999; Sweller, Ayres, & Kalyuga, 2011). Extraneous processing is cognitive processing during learning that does not support the instructional goal and is caused by poor instructional design, such as placing text describing a figure on one page and placing the figure several pages later.

Extraneous processing does not involve any of the cognitive processes for meaningful learning shown in figure 7.3 (i.e., no selecting, organizing, or integrating). Essential processing is cognitive processing during learning that

Table 7.1. Three Demands on the Learner's Cognitive Capacity during Learning

Name	Description	Cause
Extraneous processing →	cognitive processing that does not support the instructional goal	→ caused by poor design of instruction
Essential processing →	cognitive processing needed to mentally represent the material (i.e., selecting and initial organizing)	→ caused by the inherent complexity of the material
Generative processing →	deeper cognitive processing needed to make sense of the material (i.e., organizing and integrating)	→ caused by the learner's motivation to understand

is needed to mentally represent the material and is caused by the complexity of the material for the learner, such as teaching middle school students about how lightning develops.

The underlying processes (as shown in figure 7.3) are selecting relevant information and organizing it as presented. Generative processing is deeper cognitive processing during learning aimed at making sense of the material and is caused by the learner's motivation to understand, such as when a learner explains the material to himself. The underlying processes are organizing incoming material into pictorial and verbal representations, and integrating the representations with each other and with relevant prior knowledge activated from long-term memory.

Figure 7.4 summarizes three kinds of instructional scenarios—*extraneous overload*, *essential overload*, and *generative underutilization*. In extraneous overload, poor instructional design causes learners to engage in so much extraneous processing during learning that not enough cognitive capacity remains to allow the learner to engage in the required levels of essential and generative processing. The solution to this instructional problem is to redesign instruction in ways that reduce extraneous processing.

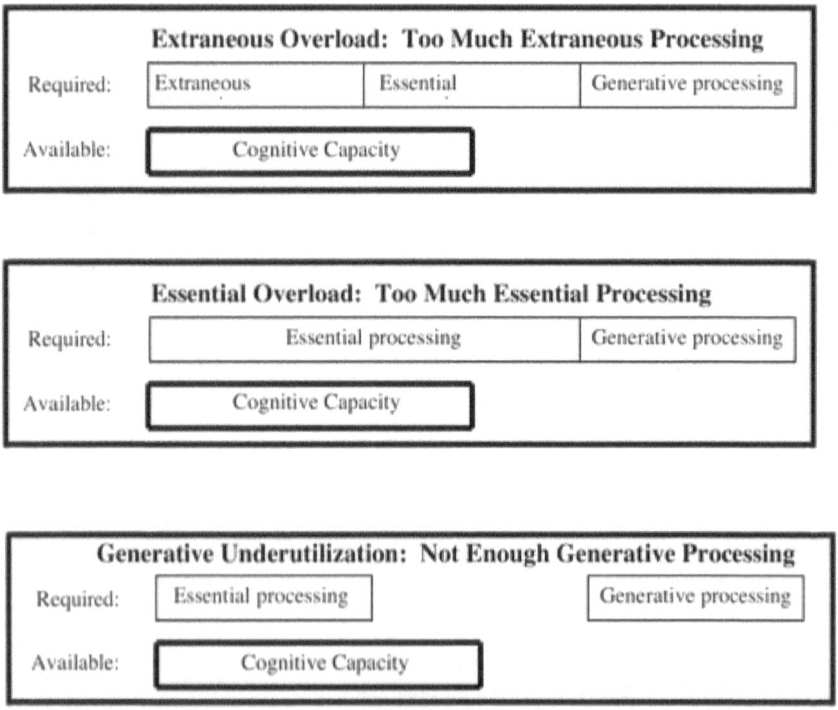

Figure 7.4.

In essential overload, the inherent complexity of the material—such as having many elements that interact with one another—causes so much essential processing that there is not enough cognitive capacity to handle all of it and the additional generative processing that is needed. Even though instruction is designed in ways that reduce extraneous processing, in this instructional problem what is needed is to redesign instruction in ways that manage essential processing.

Finally, in generative overutilization, we may have designed instruction in ways that reduce extraneous processing and manage essential processing so the learner has sufficient cognitive capacity available, but the learner does not choose to put out the effort to engage in the level of generative processing needed to understand the material. In this case, the solution is to redesign instruction in ways that foster generative processing in the learner.

In short, effective instructional design requires research-based techniques for reducing extraneous processing, managing essential processing, and fostering generative processing.

WHICH INSTRUCTIONAL METHODS WORK BEST IN DESIGNING MULTIMEDIA INSTRUCTION?

In your role as a creator or consumer of multimedia instructional materials, you may wish to consider instructional features that reduce extraneous processing for your students, manage essential processing for your students, and foster generative processing in your students. In this section, I summarize the fruits of more than twenty years of research that compares the transfer test performance of students who learn from a standard multimedia lesson versus a modified multimedia lesson that contains one additional instructional feature.

Table 7.2 lists four principles for reducing extraneous processing and their supporting evidence (Mayer, 2005b, 2013). First, consider a slideshow presentation that uses line drawings and on-screen text to explain how a virus

Table 7.2. Four Principles for Reducing Extraneous Processing

Principle		Description		Number of tests	Median effect size
Coherence	→	reduce extraneous materials	→	14	0.97
Signaling	→	highlight essential materials	→	6	0.52
Spatial contiguity	→	place printed words near corresponding part of graphics	→	13	1.08
Temporal Contiguity	→	present corresponding narration and graphics simultaneously	→	8	1.31

causes a cold. You might want to spice up the lesson by adding some interesting facts about viruses, such as how the Ebola virus spreads. Alternatively, you might think it would be a good idea to add short video clips of lightning storms or background music to a computer-based lesson on how lightning storms develop. If you added these interesting but irrelevant facts or graphics, called *seductive details*, you would be violating the *coherence principle*.

As shown in the first line of table 7.2, the coherence principle is that people learn more deeply from multimedia lessons when extraneous material is eliminated from the lesson. The extraneous material can be interesting but irrelevant facts, or attention-grabbing illustrations or video clips that are directly relevant to the instructional goal, or even background music. You can see in the first row of table 7.2 that the coherence principle is upheld across fourteen experiment tests, yielding a median effect size of 0.97, which is in the high range.

For example, students performed better on transfer tests when seductive details (i.e., interesting but irrelevant facts and graphics) were deleted from an illustrated text (Harp & Mayer, 1997, Experiment 1; Harp & Mayer, 1998, Experiments 1, 2, 3, and 4) or a narrated animation (Mayer, Heiser, & Lonn, 2001, Experiment 3) on lightning formation.

Students performed better on transfer tests if extraneous words were eliminated from lessons containing printed text and illustrations on ocean waves (Mayer & Jackson, 2005, Experiments 1a and 1b) or lightning (Mayer, et al., 1996, Experiments 1, 2, and 3), or lessons containing narration and animation on ocean waves (Mayer & Jackson, 2005, Experiment 2); and students performed better on transfer tests when background music was deleted from computer-based narration and animation on lightning (Moreno & Mayer, 2000a, Experiment 1) or brakes (Moreno & Mayer, 2000a, Experiment 2).

The theoretical explanation is that the extraneous material encourages the learner to engage in extraneous processing, so eliminating that extraneous processing allows the learner to have more cognitive capacity available for essential processing and generative processing. If you can't eliminate irrelevant material from a lesson, the next best approach can be to highlight the relevant material. As shown in the second row of table 7.2, the *signaling principle* is that people learn more deeply when essential material in a lesson is highlighted.

The highlighting can include the use of headings, bold font, and outlines. The signaling principle was supported across six experimental tests, yielding a median effect size of 0.52, which is a medium-sized effect. Transfer test performance was higher for signaled versus non-signaled lessons involving a computer-based multimedia lesson on how airplanes achieve lift (Mautone & Mayer, 2001, Experiments 3a and 3b) and paper-based lessons on lightning (Harp & Mayer, 1998, Experiment 3a) and biology (Stull & Mayer, 2007,

Experiments 1, 2, and 3). As boundary conditions, signaling may be more effective when the display is complex (Jueng, Chandler, & Sweller, 1997) and when it used sparingly (Stull & Mayer, 2007).

Let's see what happens when you have a lesson containing graphics and printed text. A common practice is to place the text in a caption at the bottom of the screen or figure. However, this seemingly reasonable approach violates the *spatial contiguity principle*, which states that people learn more deeply when printed words are placed next to corresponding parts of the visual display. Instead of putting printed words at the bottom of the screen as a caption, the spatial contiguity principle calls for moving each segment of words next to the part of the graphic it describes.

As shown in the third row of table 7.2, support for the spatial contiguity principle comes from thirteen experimental comparisons, in which the median effect size was 1.08, which is a large effect. Evidence for spatial contiguity comes from paper-based lessons on lighting (Mayer, Steinhoff, Bower, & Mars, 1995, Experiments 1, 2, and 3), brakes (Mayer, 1989, Experiment 2), the heart (Chandler & Sweller, 1991, Experiment 6), engineering (Chandler & Sweller, 1991, Experiment 1; Chandler & Sweller, 1992, Experiment 1; Tindall-Ford, Chandler, & Sweller, 1997, Experiment 1).

Evidence also comes from mathematics (Sweller, Chandler, Tierney, & Cooper, 1990, Experiment 1); and computer-based lessons on lightning (Moreno & Mayer, 1999b, Experiment 1), pumps (Bodemer, Ploetzner, Feuerlein, & Spada, 2004, Experiment 1), statistics (Bodemer, Ploetzner, Feuerlein, & Spada, 2004, Experiment 2), and physics (Kester, Kirschner, & van Merriënboer, 2005, Experiment 1).

Reviews of the spatial contiguity effect (Ayres & Sweller, 2005; Ginns, 2006) also have found strong supporting evidence, but the spatial contiguity principle may apply most strongly for low-knowledge learners (Kalyuga, 2005), when the material is complicated (Ayres & Sweller, 2005), and when the learner places the words next to graphics through interactivity (Bodemer, Ploetzner, Feuerlein, & Spada, 2004).

Next, consider a situation in which you have an animation (or series of still slides) that shows how the human respiratory system works along with a narration that describes how the human respiratory system works. You might think it would be a good idea to present the narration first, followed by the graphics or vice versa, because this gives the learner two exposures to the materials. However, based on the *temporal contiguity principle*, summarized in the fourth line of table 7.2, you would be wrong in presenting graphics and narration successively.

The temporal contiguity principle states that people learn more deeply when corresponding graphics and narration are presented simultaneously rather than successively. In eight out of eight experimental comparisons, students performed better on transfer tests when they received graphics and narration simultaneously rather than successively, yielding a median effect size of $d = 1.31$.

The temporal contiguity effect was found for animation and narration concerning tire pumps (Mayer & Anderson, 1991, Experiments 1 and 2a; Mayer & Anderson, 1992, Experiment 2; Mayer & Sims, 1994, Experiment 1), car brakes (Mayer & Anderson, 1992, Experiment 2; Mayer, Moreno, Boire, & Vagge, 1999, Experiment 2), lungs (Mayer & Sims, 1994, Experiment 2), and lightning (Mayer, Moreno, Boire, & Vagge. 1999, Experiment 1).

The theoretical rationale is that learners given successive presentations are not able to hold the words in working memory until they see the graphics (or vice versa), so they are less likely to make mental connections between corresponding words and pictures. The temporal contiguity principle may not apply when the lesson is broken into short segments or when the pace and order of the lesson can be controlled by the learner (Mayer, 2009).

Table 7.3 lists three principles for managing essential processing and summarizes supporting evidence (Mayer, 2005c, 2013). What should you do when you have to explain complicated material that may overload the learner's working memory? You can't cut out some of the material because it is essential for explaining the material. One useful approach summarized is to break the lesson into smaller parts.

As summarized in the top row of table 3, the *segmenting principle* states that people learn more deeply when a multimedia presentation is broken into manageable segments that the learner can initiate. For example, in a segmented lesson, a narrated animation may be broken into shorter segments that can be started by clicking a button. In nine experimental comparisons, students who received segmented lessons performed better on transfer tests than did students who received continuous lessons, yielding a median effect size of $d = 0.82$, which is a large effect.

The segmenting principle was found in computer-based multimedia lessons on electric motors (Mayer, Dow, & Mayer, 2003, Experiments 2a and

Table 7.3. Three Principles for Managing Essential Processing

Principle	Description	Number of tests	Median effect size
Segmenting →	break material into manageable segments →	9	0.82
Pretraining →	provide pretraining in names and characteristics of key terms →	10	0.88
Modality →	use spoken words rather than printed words →	32	0.88

2b), lightning (Mayer & Chandler, 2001, Experiment 2), geography (Mautone & Mayer, 2007, Experiment 2), chemistry (Lee, Plass, & Homer, 2006, Experiment 1), and probability problem solving (Gerjets, Scheiter, & Catrambone, 2006, Experiments 1a and 1b); and a paper-based mathematics lesson (Ayres, 2006, Experiments 1a and 2a). The theoretical explanation is that the learner is better able to completely process the multimedia lesson when the material is presented in a series of bite-size chunks.

A similar approach to managing essential processing is to make sure the learner knows the key terms before you present a multimedia lesson that contains those terms. In the second row of table 7.3, the *pretraining principle* states that people learn more deeply from a multimedia lesson when they receive pretraining in the names and characteristics of the key concepts in the lesson.

For example, before receiving a narrated animation on how a car's braking system works, students may be able click on each part (such as a piston or brake shoe) and get the name and characteristics of the part. In ten experimental comparisons, students who received pretraining performed better on transfer tests after a multimedia lesson than did students who did not, yielding a median effect size of $d = 0.88$, which is a large effect.

The pretraining principle has been supported in studies involving computer-based presentations on brakes (Mayer, Mathias, & Wetzell, 2002, Experiments 1 and 2), pumps (Mayer, Mathias, & Wetzell, 2002, Experiment 3), statistics (Kester, Kirschner, & van Merriënboer, 2004, Experiment 1), and electronics (Kester, Kirschner, & van Merriënboer, 2006, Experiment 1).

Support also comes from studies on computer-based simulation games in geology (Mayer, Mautone, & Prothero, 2002, Experiments 2 and 3); and paper-based multimedia lessons on mathematics (Clarke, Ayres, & Sweller, 2005, Experiment 1a) and electrical engineering (Pollock, Chandler, & Sweller, 2002, Experiments 1 and 2). The theoretical rationale is that learners can devote more cognitive resources to building connections among the key concepts in the lesson if they already know what the key concepts mean.

You might suppose that it does not matter whether a multimedia lesson expresses words in printed form or spoken form, but according to the *modality principle* you would be wrong. In the third line in table 7.3, the modality principle states that people learn better from a multimedia lesson when the words are in spoken form rather than printed form. In thirty-six experimental comparisons—the most of any principle—people tended to learn better from multimedia lessons that contained spoken words rather than printed words, yielding a median effect size of $d = 0.88$, which is a large effect.

The modality effect has been tested by comparing computer-based multimedia lessons with recorded voice or on-screen text (Atkinson, 2002, Experiments 1a, 1b, and 2; Craig, Gholson, & Driscoll, 2002, Experiment

2; Harskamp, Mayer, Suhre, & Jansma, 2007, Experiments 1 and 2a; Jeung, Chandler, & Sweller, 1997, Experiments 1, 2, and 3; Kalyuga, Chandler, & Sweller, 1999, Experiment 1; Kalyuga, Chandler, & Sweller, 2000, Experiment 1; Mayer, Dow, & Mayer, 2003, Experiment 1; Mayer & Moreno, 1998, Experiments 1 and 2; Moreno & Mayer, 1999b, Experiments 1 and 2; Tabbers, Martens, & van Merriënboer, 2004, Experiment 1).

The modality effect has also been tested by comparing paper-based multimedia lessons with tape-recorded voice or printed text (Leahy, Chandler, & Sweller, 2003, Experiment 1; Mousavi, Low, & Sweller, 1995, Experiments 1, 2, 3, 4, and 5; Tindall-Ford, Chandler, & Sweller, 1997, Experiments 1, 2, and 3), and computer-based multimedia simulation games with spoken text or on-screen text (Moreno & Mayer, 2002, Experiments 1a, 1b, 1c, 2a, and 2b; Moreno, Mayer, Spires, & Lester, 2001, Experiments 4a, 4b, 5a, and 5b; O'Neil, Mayer, Herl, Niemi, Olin, & Thurman, 2000, Experiment 1).

Similarly, strong support for the modality effect has been reported in recent reviews (Ginns, 2005; Low & Sweller, 2005; Mayer, 2005c). There are some potential boundary conditions, consistent with the cognitive theory shown in figure 2, in which the modality principle is strongest when the material is complex for the learner (Tindall-Ford, Chandler, & Sweller, 1997) and when the pace is fast and not under learner control (Tabbers, Martens, & van Merriënboer, 2004).

The theoretical explanation is that people can't pay attention to the visual display when they are reading a caption and they can't pay attention to printed words when they are paying attention to the visual display. Thus, using spoken text helps offload verbal processing to the verbal channel, thereby freeing up capacity in the visual channel for the visual material.

Table 7.4 describes three principles for fostering generative processing and summarizes supporting evidence (Mayer, 2005d), all of which attempt to make the communication feel more like a personal conversation between the teacher and the learner. In the top row, the *personalization principle* states

Table 7.4. Three Principles for Fostering Generative Processing

Principle		Description		Number of tests	Median effect size
Personalization	→	put words in conversational style rather than formal style	→	11	1.11
Embodiment	→	jave instructors use human-like gesturing rather than no gesturing	→	3	0.92
Voice	→	use human speech rather than machine speech	→	3	0.78

that people try harder to understand a lesson when the words are in conversational style rather than formal style. For example, conversational style involves using first and second person such as "I" and "you" whereas formal style uses third-person constructions.

In eleven experimental comparisons, students performed better on a transfer test when the words in a multimedia lesson were in conversational style rather than in formal style, yielding a median effect size of $d = 1.11$, which is a large effect. The personalization effect was found in learning about lightning in a computer-based multimedia presentation (Moreno & Mayer, 2000b, Experiments 1 and 2) and the human respiratory system in a computer-based multimedia presentation (Mayer, Fennell, Farmer, & Campbell, 2004, Experiments 1, 2, and 3).

Personalization effect was also found in learning botany in a multimedia game (Moreno & Mayer, 2000b, Experiments, 3, 4, and 5; Moreno & Mayer, 2004, Experiments 1a and 1b), and engineering in a multimedia game (Wang, Johnson, Mayer, Rizzo, Shaw, & Collins, 2008, Experiment 1). The rationale for the personalization effect is that social cues such as conversational speech can prime a social stance in learners, which causes them to feel compelled to try to comprehend what a communication partner is saying.

In the second row of table 7.4, the *embodiment principle* states that students learn more deeply when the instructor or on-screen agent displays human-like gesturing rather than not gesturing. In three experimental comparisons, students performed better on a transfer test after viewing a slideshow on how solar cells work.

The slide show provided viewing in which an on-screen agent engaged in human-like gesturing, facial expressions, eye gaze, and body movement than when the on-screen agent stood still (Mayer & DaPra, 2012, Experiments 1, 2, and 3), yielding a median effect size of $d = 0.92$, which is a large effect. The theoretical explanation is that when the instructor displays social cues such as human-like gesturing, the students are more likely to accept the instructor as a communication partner and therefore try harder to make sense of what the agent is saying.

In the third row of table 7.4, the *voice principle* states that people learn better when spoken text involves a human voice rather than a machine-generated voice. In three experimental comparisons involving computer-based lessons on lightning (Mayer, Sobko, & Mautone, 2003, Experiment 2) and mathematics word problems (Atkinson, Mayer, & Merrill, 2005, Experiments 1 and 2), students performed better on transfer tests from multimedia lessons with human voice rather than machine voice, yielding a median effect size of $d = 0.78$, which is a large effect.

The theoretical explanation is that a human voice is a social cue that primes a social stance in learners so they are more likely to view the on-screen agent as a communication partner. Thus, they feel compelled to try harder to understand what their communication partner is saying.

CONCLUSION

Multimedia instruction has potential to improve student learning, but it is most effective when designed in light of research-based theories of how people learn from words and pictures and grounded in research-based principles. You can improve your effectiveness as a creator or consumer of multimedia instructional materials by understanding how to guide the cognitive processes that lead to meaningful learning (i.e., selecting, organizing, and integrating) and understanding how features of multimedia instruction can reduce extraneous processing, manage essential processing, and foster generative processing.

As advances in technology bring ever more spectacular opportunities—ranging from educational games to on-screen pedagogical agents, from intelligent tutoring systems to virtual reality—your instructional decisions still should be based on your core understanding of how students learn and what works based on empirical research.

AUTHOR NOTE

Preparation of this chapter was supported by a grant from the Office of Naval Research. This research evidence in this chapter in the section titled "Which Instructional Methods Work Best in Designing Multimedia Instruction?" is based on Mayer (2013).

REFERENCES

Atkinson, R. K. (2002). Optimizing learning from examples using animated pedagogical agents. *Journal of Educational Psychology, 94*, 416–427.

Atkinson, R. K., Mayer, R. E., & Merrill, M. M. (2005). Fostering social agency in multimedia learning: Examining the impact of an animated agent's voice. *Contemporary Educational Psychology, 30*, 117–139.

Ayres, P. (2006). Impact of reducing intrinsic cognitive load on learning in a mathematical domain. *Applied Cognitive Psychology, 20*, 287–298.

Ayres, P., & Sweller, J. (2005). The split attention principle in multimedia learning. In R. E. Mayer (Ed.), *The Cambridge handbook of multimedia learning* (pp. 135–146). New York, NY: Cambridge University Press.

Baddeley, A. D. (1999). *Human memory*. Boston, MA: Allyn & Bacon.

Bodemer, D., Ploetzner, R., Feuerlein, I., & Spada, H. (2004). The active integration of information during learning with dynamic and interactive visualisations. *Learning and Instruction, 14*, 325–341.

Chandler, P., & Sweller, J. (1991). Cognitive load theory and the format of instruction. *Cognition and Instruction, 8*, 293–332.

Chandler, P., & Sweller, J. (1992). The split-attention effect as a factor in the design of instruction. *British Journal of Educational Psychology, 62*, 233–246.

Clarke, T., Ayres, P., & Sweller, J. (2005). The impact of sequencing and prior knowledge on learning mathematics through spreadsheet applications. *Educational Technology Research and Development, 53*, 15–24.

Cohen, J. (1988). *Statistical power analysis for the behavioral sciences.* Mahwah, NJ: Erlbaum.

Craig, S. D., Gholson, B., & Driscoll, D. M. (2002). Animated pedagogical agents in multimedia educational environments: Effects of agent properties, picture features, and redundancy. *Journal of Educational Psychology, 94*, 428–434.

Fletcher, J. D., & Tobias, S. (2005). The multimedia principle. In R. E. Mayer (Ed.), *The Cambridge handbook of multimedia learning* (pp. 117–134). New York, NY: Cambridge University Press.

Gerjets, P., Scheiter, K., & Catrambone, R. (2006). Can learning from molar and modular worked examples be enhanced by providing instructional explanations and prompting self-explanations? *Learning and Instruction, 16*, 104–121.

Ginns, P. (2005). Meta-analysis of the modality effect. *Learning and Instruction, 15*, 313–332.

Ginns, P. (2006). Integrating information: A meta-analysis of spatial contiguity and temporal contiguity effects. *Learning and Instruction, 16*, 511–525.

Harp, S. F., & Mayer, R. E. (1997). The role of interest in learning from scientific text and illustrations: On the distinction between emotional interest and cognitive interest. *Journal of Educational Psychology, 89*, 92–102.

Harp, S. F., & Mayer, R. E. (1998). How seductive details do their damage: A theory of cognitive interest in science learning. *Journal of Educational Psychology, 90*, 414–434.

Harskamp, E., Mayer, R. E., Suhre, C., & Jansma, J. (2007). Does the modality principle for multimedia learning apply to science classrooms? *Learning and Instruction, 18*, 465–477.

Hattie, J. (2009). *Visible learning.* New York, NY: Routledge.

Jeung, H., Chandler, P., & Sweller, J. (1997). The role of visual indicators in dual sensory mode instruction. *Educational Psychology, 17*, 329–433.

Kalyuga, S. (2005). Prior knowledge principle in multimedia learning. In R. E. Mayer (Ed.), *The Cambridge handbook of multimedia learning* (pp. 325–338). New York, NY: Cambridge University Press.

Kalyuga, S., Chandler, P., & Sweller, J. (1999). Managing split-attention and redundancy in multimedia instruction. *Applied Cognitive Psychology, 13*, 351–371.

Kalyuga, S., Chandler, P., & Sweller, J. (2000). Incorporating learner experience into the design of multimedia instruction. *Journal of Educational Psychology, 92*, 126–136.

Kester, L., Kirschner, P. A., & van Merriënboer, J. G. G. (2004). Timing of information presentation in learning statistics. *Instructional Science, 32*, 233–252.

Kester, L., Kirschner, P. A., & van Merriënboer, J. J. G. (2005). The management of cognitive load during complex cognitive skill acquisition by means of computer-simulated problem solving. *British Journal of Educational Psychology, 75*, 71–85.

Kester, L., Kirschner, P. A., & van Merriënboer, J. J. G (2006). Just-in-time information presentation: Improving learning a troubleshooting skill. *Contemporary Educational Psychology, 31*, 167–185.

Leahy, W., Chandler, P., & Sweller, J. (2003). When auditory presentations should and should not be a component of multimedia instruction. *Applied Cognitive Psychology, 17*, 401–418.

Lee, H., Plass, J. L., & Homer, B. D. (2006). Optimizing cognitive load for learning from computer-based science simulations. *Journal of Educational Psychology, 98*, 902–913.

Low, R., & Sweller, J. (2005). The modality principle in multimedia learning. In R. E. Mayer (Ed.), *The Cambridge handbook of multimedia learning* (pp. 147–158). New York, NY: Cambridge University Press.

Mautone, P. D., & Mayer, R. E. (2001). Signaling as a cognitive guide in multimedia learning. *Journal of Educational Psychology, 93*, 377–389.

Mautone, P. D., & Mayer, R. E. (2007). Cognitive aids for guiding graph comprehension. *Journal of Educational Psychology, 99*, 640–652.

Mayer, R. E. (1989). Systematic thinking fostered by illustrations in scientific text. *Journal of Educational Psychology, 81*, 240–246.

Mayer, R. E. (Ed.). (2005a). *The Cambridge handbook of multimedia learning.* New York, NY: Cambridge University Press.

Mayer, R. E. (2005b). Principles for reducing extraneous processing in multimedia learning: Coherence, signaling, redundancy, spatial contiguity, and temporal contiguity principles. In R. E. Mayer (Ed.), *The Cambridge handbook of multimedia learning* (pp. 183–200). New York, NY: Cambridge University Press.

Mayer, R. E. (2005c). Principles for managing essential processing in multimedia learning: Segmenting, pretraining, and modality principles. In R. E. Mayer (Ed.), *The Cambridge handbook of multimedia learning* (pp. 169–182). New York, NY: Cambridge University Press.

Mayer, R. E. (2005d). Principles of multimedia learning based on social cues: Personalization, voice, and image principles. In R. E. Mayer (Ed.), *The Cambridge handbook of multimedia learning* (pp. 201–212). New York, NY: Cambridge University Press.

Mayer, R. E. (2009). *Multimedia learning* (2nd ed.). New York, NY: Cambridge University Press.

Mayer, R. E. (2011a). Instruction based on visualizations. In R. E. Mayer & P. A. Alexander (Eds.), *Handbook of research on learning and instruction* (pp. 427–445). New York, NY: Routledge.

Mayer, R. E. (2011b). *Applying the science of learning.* Upper Saddle River, NJ: Pearson.

Mayer, R. E. (2013). Fostering learning with visual displays. In G. Schraw, M. McCrudden, & D. Robinson (Eds.), *Learning through visual displays*. Charlotte, NC: Information Age Publishing.

Mayer, R. E., & Anderson, R. B. (1991). Animations need narrations: An experimental test of a dual-coding hypothesis. *Journal of Educational Psychology, 83*, 484–490.

Mayer, R. E., & Anderson, R. B. (1992). The instructive animation: Helping students build connections between words and pictures in multimedia learning. *Journal of Educational Psychology, 84*, 444–452.

Mayer, R. E., Bove, W., Bryman, A., Mars, R., & Tapangco, L. (1996). When less is more: Meaningful learning from visual and verbal summaries of science textbook lessons. *Journal of Educational Psychology, 88*, 64–73.

Mayer, R. E., & Chandler, P. (2001). When learning is just a click away: Does simple user interaction foster deeper understanding of multimedia messages? *Journal of Educational Psychology, 93*, 390–397.

Mayer, R. E., & DaPra, C. S. (2012). An embodiment effect in computer-based learning with animated pedagogical agents. *Journal of Experimental Psychology: Applied, 18*(3), 239–252.

Mayer, R. E., Dow, G., & Mayer, R. E. (2003). Multimedia learning in an interactive self-explaining environment: What works in the design of agent-based microworlds? *Journal of Educational Psychology, 95*, 806–813.

Mayer, R. E., Fennell, S., Farmer, L., & Campbell, J. (2004). A personalization effect in multimedia learning: Students learn better when words are in conversational style rather than formal style. *Journal of Educational Psychology, 96*, 389–395.

Mayer, R. E., & Gallini, J. K. (1990). When is an illustration worth ten thousand words? *Journal of Educational Psychology, 82*, 715–726.

Mayer, R. E., Heiser, H., & Lonn, S. (2001). Cognitive constraints on multimedia learning: When presenting more material results in less understanding. *Journal of Educational Psychology, 93*, 187–198.

Mayer, R. E., & Jackson, J. (2005). The case for conciseness in scientific explanations: Quantitative details can hurt qualitative understanding. *Journal of Experimental Psychology: Applied, 11*, 13–18.

Mayer, R. E., Mathias, A., & Wetzell, K. (2002). Fostering understanding of multimedia messages through pre-training: Evidence for a two-stage theory of mental model construction. *Journal of Experimental Psychology: Applied, 8*, 147–154.

Mayer, R. E., Mautone, P., & Prothero, W. (2002). Pictorial aids for learning by doing in a multimedia geology simulation game. *Journal of Educational Psychology, 94*, 171–185.

Mayer, R. E., & Moreno, R. E. (1998). A split-attention effect in multimedia learning: Evidence for dual processing systems in working memory. *Journal of Educational Psychology, 90*, 312–320.

Mayer, R. E., Moreno, R., Boire, M., & Vagge, S. (1999). Maximizing constructivist learning from multimedia communications by minimizing cognitive load. *Journal of Educational Psychology, 91*, 638–643.

Mayer, R. E., & Sims, V. K. (1994). For whom is a picture worth a thousand words? Extensions of a dual-coding theory of multimedia learning. *Journal of Educational Psychology, 84,* 389–401.

Mayer, R. E., Sobko, K., & Mautone, P. D. (2003). Social cues in multimedia learning: Role of speaker's voice. *Journal of Educational Psychology, 95,* 419–425.

Mayer, R. E., Steinhoff, K., Bower, G., & Mars, R. (1995). A generative theory of textbook design: Using annotated illustrations to foster meaningful learning of science text. *Educational Technology Research and Development, 43,* 31–43.

Moreno, R., & Mayer, R. E. (1999a). Multimedia-supported metaphors for meaning making in mathematics. *Cognition and Instruction, 17,* 215–248.

Moreno, R., & Mayer, R. E. (1999b). Cognitive principles of multimedia learning: The role of modality and contiguity. *Journal of Educational Psychology, 91,* 358–368.

Moreno, R., & Mayer, R. E. (2000a). A coherence effect in multimedia learning: The case for minimizing irrelevant sounds in the design of multimedia messages. *Journal of Educational Psychology, 92,* 117–125.

Moreno, R., & Mayer, R. E. (2000b). Engaging students in active learning: The case for personalized multimedia messages. *Journal of Educational Psychology, 92,* 724–733.

Moreno, R., & Mayer, R. E. (2002a). Learning science in virtual reality multimedia environments: Role of methods and media. *Journal of Educational Psychology, 94,* 598–610.

Moreno, R., & Mayer, R. E. (2002b). Verbal redundancy in multimedia learning: When reading helps listening. *Journal of Educational Psychology, 94,* 156–163.

Moreno, R., & Mayer, R. E. (2004). Personalized messages that promote science learning in virtual environments. *Journal of Educational Psychology, 96,* 165–173.

Moreno, R., Mayer, R. E., Spires, H. A., & Lester, J. C. (2001). The case for social agency in computer-based teaching: Do students learn more deeply when they interact with animated pedagogical agents? *Cognition and Instruction, 19,* 177–213.

Mousavi, S. Y., Low, R., & Sweller, J. (1995). Reducing cognitive load by mixing auditory and visual presentation modes. *Journal of Educational Psychology, 87,* 319–334.

O'Neil, H. F. (2005). *What works in distance learning: Guidelines.* Greenwich, CT: Information Age Publishing.

O'Neil, H. F., Mayer, R. E., Herl, H. E., Niemi, C., Olin, K., & Thurman, R. A. (2000). Instructional strategies for virtual aviation training environments. In H. F. O'Neil & D. H. Andrews (Eds.), *Aircrew training and assessment* (pp. 105–130). Mahwah, NJ: Erlbaum.

Paivio, A. (1986). *Mental representations: A dual-coding approach.* Oxford, UK: Oxford University Press.

Paivio, A. (2007). *Mind and its evolution: A dual-coding approach.* Mahwah, NJ: Erlbaum.

Pollock, E., Chandler, P., & Sweller, J. (2002). Assimilating complex information. *Learning and Instruction, 12,* 61–86.

Stull, A., & Mayer, R. E. (2007). Learning by doing versus learning by viewing: Three experimental comparisons of learner-generated versus author-provided graphic organizers. *Journal of Educational Psychology, 99*, 808–820.

Sweller, J. (1999). *Instructional design in technical areas.* Camberwell, Australia: ACER Press.

Sweller, J., Ayres, P., & Kalyuga, S. (2011). *Cognitive load theory.* New York, NY: Springer.

Sweller, J., Chandler, P., Tierney, P., & Cooper, M. (1990). Cognitive load and selective attention as factors in the structuring of technical material. *Journal of Experimental Psychology: General, 119*, 176–192.

Tabbers, H. K., Martens, R. L., & van Merriënboer, J. J. G. (2004). Multimedia instruction and cognitive load theory: Effects of modality and cueing. *British Journal of Educational Psychology, 74*, 71–81.

Tindall-Ford, S., Chandler, P., & Sweller, J. (1997). When two sensory modalities are better than one. *Journal of Experimental Psychology: Applied, 3*, 257–287.

Wang, N., Johnson, W. L., Mayer, R. E., Rizzo, P., Shaw, E., & Collins, H. (2008). The politeness effect: Pedagogical agents and learning outcomes. *International Journal of Human Computer Studies, 66*, 96–112.

Wittrock, M. C. (1989). Generative processes of comprehension. *Educational Psychologist, 24*, 345–376.

Chapter 8

Next Generation Teachers: Integrating Multimedia Learning into Teacher Preparation

Patrick M. Jenlink

INTRODUCTION

We live in a multimedia-enriched world, surrounded by complex images, movements, sounds, and representations, where multimedia literacy is becoming ever more important. The rapid advancement of multimedia in an increasingly digital world and its applications in educational contexts are changing the spatial dynamics of teaching and learning in higher education, particularly teacher education. Understanding the students' culture, experiences, and knowledge of the world is essential to critical and effective teaching. The role that media and digital technologies play in learning activities in higher education has dramatically increased, from interaction with online learning communities and virtual worlds to multimedia learning[1] as a critical part of the learning architecture that connects students with teachers. Within higher education and K–12 education alike, Bartow (2014) notes that "media interrupt formal education in multiple ways" (p. 36). Prevailing constructions of school, of teacher and students, and of teaching and learning are challenged.

Multimedia learning presents critical educational, ethical, and revolutionary challenges to the organization and structure of schools. They catalyze, as Bartow (2014) argues, "a fundamental examination of what public education should look like and be like in a democracy" (p. 37). Considering the level of social engagement in media-enriched spaces today, the disparity between what happens inside and outside the classroom, both in higher education and K–12 educational settings, seems especially problematic. Saltmarsh and Sunderland-Smith (2010), in considering the implications of social media, make the point that critical aspects of this dramatic shift involve challenges to not just the "how" but also the "who" of teaching (p. 15).

Multimedia-enriched learning incorporates multiple forms of text, audio, graphics, animation, or video to convey information. Mayer (2003) explains that multimedia learning

> occurs when students build mental representations from words and pictures that are presented to them (e.g., printed text and illustrations or narration and animation). The promise of multimedia learning is that students can learn more deeply from well-designed multi-media messages consisting of words and pictures than from more traditional modes of communication involving words alone. (p. 125)

Multimedia learning transforms the teacher's understanding of pedagogical strategies and curricula, evolving from a largely linear learning environment based on textbooks to an increasingly nonlinear environment defined by multiple forms of media (Mayer, 2005a). Multimedia-enriched learning affords students a strong degree of choice as they pursue learning with multimedia texts. Multimedia offers classroom teachers multiple ways of engaging students in the learning process; however, multimedia approaches to teaching and learning also present challenges for teachers (Lambert & Cuper, 2008).

Jenkins, Clinton, Purushotma, et al. (2009) have argued that outside of schools, youth are actively involved in a "participatory culture . . . that cuts across educational practices, creative processes, community life, and democratic citizenship" (p. 9). The importance of this point lies in the realization that within schools, participatory culture is often non-prevalent. The "how" and the "who" of teaching are defined very differently in the school setting than what is experienced outside the school setting. For youth today, social media present a participatory culture that has low barriers to civic engagement and creative expression with strong support for sharing creative work and a ready informal system of mentorship whereby more experienced members pass on knowledge to novices (Jenkins, et al., 2009).

Preparing teachers to address the "how" and the "who" of teaching in relation to needs of a generation of youth growing up in media-enriched environments draws specific attention to how we advantage teacher preparation by embracing multimedia learning as a cognitive and pedagogical interface between the student and teacher in a world rapidly changing in concert with the influence and evolution of social media technologies. With this in mind, three major issues confront teacher education today, in consideration of preparing teachers for the new generation of youth entering schools today and in ensuring that teacher educators are ready for the next generation of teacher education students entering college.

MAJOR ISSUES TO CONSIDER

One of the major issues confronting teacher education in colleges and universities, and simultaneously impacting the pre-K–12 classroom teacher's practice, is the rapidly evolving influence of Web 2.0 social media on the generation of students preparing to and/or entering schools and universities. Society's educational systems are being redefined by the ideological and technological foundations of Web 2.0,[2] which "allow the creation and exchange of user-generated content" (Kaplan & Haenlein, 2010, p. 61). Social media create highly interactive platforms through which individuals and communities share, cocreate, discuss, and modify user-generated content. They introduce substantial and pervasive changes to communication between organizations, communities, and individuals.

A second major issue confronting teacher education is the "digital divide,"[3] a divide that separates teachers and students, a "digital technology" divide influenced by social media that students inherently and intuitively incorporate into their lives. Students grow up today living in a social media–enriched environment that is often unfamiliar to teachers who were prepared to teach in preparation programs absent the ideological and technological influences of Web 2.0. Both positive and negative aspects of social media work to shape social interaction in society and in educational settings. As Prensky (2001) argued more than a decade ago, "our students have changed. Today's students are no longer the people our educational systems were designed to teach" (p. 1). The social media phenomenon is important in the sense that society—and its educational systems—is influenced by shifting paradigms of technology/social media and how these paradigms affect the interface between teacher preparation and practice, between the success of teachers in the classroom/school and the success of teacher educators in colleges/universities preparing teachers.

Equally important is the success of the student. The student, characterized by Prensky (2001) as a "digital native," is now characterized as a "neomillennial user" (Baird & Fisher, 2006). The "neomillennial" generation of youth in society is experiencing a digital evolution in technology that sets that generation further apart from the pre-millennial and millennial generations of just a few years ago. Web 2.0 has shifted the calculus of technology in education, making social media a critical variable in student learning and knowledge acquisition. The implications of the neomillennial generation of youth for teacher education are yet to be fully realized, but teacher educators cannot be differential in their positions on the myriad forms of social media that are emerging and evolving. As the calculus of technology has shifted, so too has the digital divide, and teacher educators are now challenged to reexamine pedagogical and curricular perspectives aligned with the "learning-to-teach" experience.

A third major issue relates to the reality that schools today often are not places where students are allowed or encouraged to engage in collaborative discussions and creation and re-creation of knowledge. Neomillennial youth today have ubiquitous access via social media to extensive collaboration in social, economic, and political, and entertainment sectors. Too infrequently, youth in school settings are distanced from the very experience of learning through social media they value, forced to experience learning absent rich social interactions and digitally enriched via social media (Ito, et al., 2008; Collins & Halverson, 2009). This distancing presents a furthering of the divide between student and teacher. And the divide is widened exponentially by the learning outside school as neomillennial youth gravitate to social media spaces and the use of Web 2.0 social media tools where knowledges, skills, and inclinations are valued more than what goes on in the school setting and classroom.

These learning experiences that neomillennial youth share outside of school are increasingly recognized as emblematic of a changing society, often within and across multiple social media platforms, necessary to participating fully in society but problematically linked to "'macro' elements of the social structure of society such as global economics, labour markets, and political and cultural institutions" (Facer & Selwyn, 2010, p. 220). For neomillennial youth, social media have become central to and are redefining many aspects of daily life—how they communicate, learn, create, and consume knowledge about their shared lives (Leu, et al., 2009). The Web 2.0 social media-animated movement presents pointed challenges to traditional notions of teaching and teacher preparation.

NEXT GENERATION STUDENTS

The next generation students entering education and schools for the first time in 2018 are the neomillennial[4] generation, sometimes called Digital Natives, Generation D, Generation M,[2] Net Generation, Ngeners, NetGeners, Generation Y, Generation Z, Gen Z, Generation 2020, Millennials, or New Millennium Learners. Born during the late 1990s to 2000, this generation of young adults is unparalleled in terms of the multimedia-enriched culture in which they were raised. They gravitate toward group activity, identify with their parents' values, and spend more time on homework and housework and less time on television than those a few years older. They're almost completely unaware of a time before the internet. They're racially and ethnically diverse, with one in five having at least one immigrant parent (Howe & Strauss, 2000). The neomillennial generation will present new and complex learning challenges for teachers, challenges related to media and digital technologies and how multimedia learning has changed the cognitive interface between members of the neomillennial generation as well as redefining the nature of cognitive interface necessary for students to learn in public school and college classrooms.

Neomillennial students are different because they don't fit into a single learner profile. Raised in a multimedia-enriched world, this generation of students doesn't remember a time without internet, social media, or advances in digital innovation that define their world. They constitute a generation that cannot be generalized. They expect both their learning environments and their future workplaces to accommodate their wide-ranging sensibilities and digital technology needs.

NEXT GENERATION TEACHERS

A growing sense is that today's youth—the neomillennial generation—use digital technologies in everyday life very differently, supporting and facilitating a set of different practices and dispositions than may have been the case a few decades ago before the advent of Web 2.0 and constantly evolving-multimedia enriched world. Teachers entering classrooms and schools for the first time are confronted with neomillennial youth who see and interact with the world digitally, through rapidly evolving forms of media and digital interfaces that represent a new form of digital universe often unfamiliar to adults. Teachers who are not prepared to meet the challenge of teaching and learning equated with the needs of neomillennial youth likely will find teaching an uncomfortable experience.

Of all the adults involved in the lives of youth today, teachers are portrayed as being some of the most "poorly placed to deal well with the social, cultural and economic changes that derive from the continuing use of . . . [multimedia and] web technologies" (Bigum & Rowan, 2008, p. 250). Teacher education programs characteristically still rely strongly "upon broadcast technologies" (p. 250) rather than new digital technologies and multimedia.

The social and pedagogical interface of teacher and student as "neomillennial user" via multimedia presents significant ideological and pedagogical challenges. Rethinking how we prepare teachers will require new vistas of multimedia technologies as well as new understandings of learning theory—which outside the educational setting are integrated seamlessly in everyday social interactions for neomillennials—and will require new understandings of forms of social interactions between the neomillennial generation and the new generation of teachers we are preparing. The multimedia nature of society offers both a challenge and an opportunity to advance the experience of learning to teach in preparation programs: the challenge lies in rethinking the very nature of learning while simultaneously reconfiguring pedagogical practices and the opportunities that emerge in advancing participatory cultures of learning, each dependent on the other.

Multimedia Literacy Considerations

Media literacy is as important for the neomillennial today as more established subjects such as English, math, and science. Media literacy is equally important for teachers entering classrooms in a multimedia-enriched world. The nature of learning is being redefined in the larger culture of society through multimedia and digital technologies (Buckingham, 2003, 2007; Buckingham, et al., 2005). The neomillennial learner, as well as the older generation of adults, acquires differing levels of media literacy through the interaction with and interface through a variety of media and digital technologies. Buckingham (2007), in examining the metaphor of media literacy, has argued the point that the metaphor

> provides one means of imagining a more coherent, and ambitious, approach. The increasing convergence of contemporary media means that we need to be addressing the skills and competencies—the multiple literacies—that are required by the whole range of contemporary forms of communication. Rather than simply adding media or digital literacy to the curriculum menu, or hiving off information and communication technology into a separate subject, we need a much broader reconceptualisation of what we mean by literacy in a world dominated by electronic media. (p. 16)

Multimedia literacy advances the media literacy metaphor to a new level of meaning and importance for the teacher educator and, by extension, in the preparation of the teacher practitioner; it advances media literacy to embrace understanding of multimedia learning as a reconceptualization of teaching and learning. Teacher educators' understanding of multimedia literacy, as metaphor for teaching through the use of multimedia as integral to teaching pedagogy and curricula, "involves the rigorous analysis of media texts, in terms of the visual and verbal languages they employ and the representations of the world they make available" (Buckingham, 2007, p. 14).

The theory of multimedia learning (Mayer, 2003, 2005b) extends the metaphor of multimedia literacy to encompass multimodal literacies that use diverse media to represent audio, gestural, graphic, spatial, visual, and tactile dimensions of communication in addition to traditional written and oral forms; we live in a world that requires a grammar of multimodality (Cope & Kalantzis, 2009). We have moved from a paper and print world of telling to a media-based and digital world of showing (Kress, 2003). We live in a world increasingly defined by multimedia learning that requires multimedia literacies (Lankshear & Knobel, 2006, 2008). Multimedia learning and literacies shape the pedagogical considerations of teachers. Pedagogical and epistemological thinking (Lotherington & Jenson, 2011) aligned with multimedia literacy ensures a level of success for teachers entering classrooms populated by neomillennials who already have levels of multimedia expertise and literacy.

Pedagogical Considerations

Capturing the attention of the neomillennial generation of youth entering schools today will require teachers who are prepared to enter a Web 2.0 multi-spatial[5] environment, an environment redefined by multimedia and digital technologies. It will require teachers who understand and embrace multimedia-based infused curricula and pedagogical practices. It will require teachers who have an understanding of how curriculum is shaped and redefined by multimedia learning and the pedagogical strategies required to transform the classroom into a multimedia learning space that interfaces the student with different media representations of knowledge. Specifically, it will require teachers who are able to speak and communicate within and through multimedia and digital technologies that serve as an interface between the teacher and his students as "neomillennial users."

And advancing a Web 2.0 orientation to pedagogy will require that teacher educators be "diligent and deliberate in the pedagogical application of social media platforms in teacher preparation courses; technologies meant for self-expression or casual communication, such as social networks, will be used for effective teaching differently than for effective living" (Depietro, 2013, p. 53). Before teacher educators can prepare teachers to embrace social media-based pedagogies, teacher educators first will need to become comfortable and practiced in social media-based pedagogies in teacher preparation courses.

Teacher educators will need to ask what teaching with social media looks like, both in terms of teacher preparation and, by extension, in terms of the teacher practitioner who will enter classrooms and schools for the first time. This question is of paramount importance and requires that teacher educators give due consideration to an equally important path of inquiry: Who is teaching today and what does that look like?

Instructional Considerations

Multimedia instruction refers to designing multimedia presentations in ways that help people build mental representations (Mayer, 2003, 2005a). Instruction, as Mayer (2011) explains in relation to multimedia learning, "is the instructor's manipulation of the learner's environment in order to foster learning. Instruction affects the learner's experience, which in turn affects the knowledge that is learned, which can be evaluated by observing the learner's performance" (p. 6). Teacher preparation is concerned, in large part, with preparing teachers who have fundamental understanding of instruction and the alignment of instruction with knowledge. As Mayer further explains, "[K]nowledge is at the heart of learning of instruction, because the goal of instruction is to promote a change in the learner's knowledge" (2011, p. 6).[6]

Multimedia instruction as "presentation messages"[7] designed to create an interface between written and visual forms of knowledge in ways that are consistent with how people learn can serve as aids to human learning (Mayer, 2003, 2011). "[There is a growing research base showing that students learn more deeply from well-designed multimedia presentations than from traditional verbal-only messages, including improved performance on tests of problem-solving transfer" (Mayer, 2003, p. 127). Consequently, understanding how multimedia learning informs the design of multimedia instruction enables teachers to "draw from the power of visual and verbal forms of expression in the service of promoting student understanding" (p. 127).

Preparing teachers with skills and knowledge of multimedia learning and instructional design that enable teachers to design learning experiences for the neomillennial generation is critical to the success of a new generation of teachers entering classrooms with a media- and digital technology-savvy student population. This will require that teacher educators first take responsibility for becoming knowledgeable about cognitive theory of multimedia learning (Mayer, 2003, 2005a, 2005b, 2011). In what historically has been a book-based environment of learning to teach, teacher educators will need to focus on what Mayer (2003) identifies as three processes integral to multimedia instruction: selecting, organizing, and integrating.

Preparing teachers to engage in multimedia instruction with an understanding of printed versus visual representations of knowledge, both of which initially enter through the learner's eyes, is critical to multimedia-based learning (Mayer, 2003). Related, teachers will need to understand what differentiates external representations of knowledge. In the first set of processes, "selecting," as Mayer (2003) explains,

> The learner must select relevant aspects of the incoming images for further processing. In addition, the learner may convert some of the printed words into

verbal representations to be processed in the verbal channel and may even convert some of the illustrations into verbal representations to be processed in the verbal channel. (pp. 129–130)

The second set of processes that teachers must understand is how to facilitate the learner in understanding "organizing" of mental representations. Mayer (2003) explains that the purpose

> is to build a coherent mental representation of the verbal material (i.e., form a verbal model) and a coherent mental representation of the visual material (i.e., form a pictorial model)—processes I call *organizing*. (p. 130)

The third set of processes "is to connections between the verbal and pictorial models and with prior knowledge—processes . . ." (Mayer, 2003, p. 130).

Understanding multimedia learning instruction and design of learning experiences focuses on the learner. Learning to teach focuses on instruction as process of designing and implementing learning. Mayer (2003) notes that the "processes of selecting, organizing, and integrating generally do not occur in a rigid linear order, but rather in an iterative fashion. Once a learning outcome has been constructed, it is stored in long-term memory for future use" (p. 130). The nonlinear nature of multimedia learning is different from what many individuals entering teacher preparation experienced as students. Teacher educators, in preparing the next generation of teachers, will need to focus on what multimedia learning means and its implications for teaching. As well, teachers will need to understand that in cognitive processing, when active learning is occurring in concert with multimedia instruction, the learner's "outcome is indexed in long-term memory in a way that allows the learner to use it to solve transfer problems" (p. 130).

As Mayer (2003, 2005a, 2005b, 2011) explains, meaningful learning, according to the cognitive theory of multimedia learning, requires all sets of processes being actively engaged for both the visual and verbal representations to be processed cognitively. Multimedia instruction design methods "that enable and promote these processes are more likely to lead to meaningful learning than instructional methods that do not" (Mayer, 2003, p. 130).

Curriculum Considerations

Some individuals, as Mayer and Massa (2003) explain, "are better at processing words and some people are better at processing pictures" (p. 833), which the authors term the visualizer–verbalize dimension of learning, which has paramount import to curriculum design. Mayer and Massa further explain that the visualizer–verbalizer dimension may be understood in three separable facets:

cognitive ability (i.e., possessing low or high spatial ability), cognitive style (i.e., thinking with words or images), and learning preference (i.e., preferring instruction with text or graphics). Cognitive ability refers to things that people are capable of doing, cognitive style refers to the ways that people process and represent information, and learning preferences refer to the ways that people like information to be presented to them. (p. 833)

Curriculum design for multimedia learning requires attention to alignment of the visualization–verbalization dimension[8] of curriculum content, alignment that focuses on presentation of text (written and spoken text) and visual elements (illustrations, static graphic images, diagrams, maps, photos, animation, movie vignettes, and related media) in close proximity. As Mayer (2003) explains, the instructional presentation of multimedia has three sets of processes including selecting, organizing, and integrating. Curricula design of multimedia for presentation, in similar fashion, must follow a similar set of processes. Teacher educators engaging in multimedia learning will find that existing program curriculum will require substantive redesign, drawing on multimedia learning theory (Mayer, 2003, 2004a, 2004b, 2005b, 2008) and aligning curricula with pedagogical and instructional strategies and practices that follow the logic of selecting, organizing, and integrating the multimedia as curricula. Further arguing the import of multimedia learning in curriculum design, Gilakjani (2012) explains that "multimedia can be used to develop a more inclusive curriculum that appeals to visual, aural and kinaesthetic learners and overcome differences in student performance that may result from different learning styles" (p. 1209).

Teacher educators, in preparing next generation teachers, "must not only know and understand the functions of different media available in a media-rich environment, they should also know when best to deploy them" (Gilakjani, 2012, p. 2010). "[I]n the construction of curriculum projects with their learners, they need to guide learners in the use of word-processing, graphics and presentation programs" (p. 2010).

Students entering teacher preparation programs do so with preconceptions, cognitive patterns, of teaching based on their K–12 and university experiences. Preparing teachers for the neomillennial generation of students they will encounter in public school classrooms requires that teacher educators work with preservice-teacher students to fully understand their own preconceptions about teaching and simultaneously work to engage preservice teacher students in exploring and understanding multimedia learning theory. As Gilakjani (p. 2012) explains, "[T]eachers have to be flexible, responding to the needs that students have, not just what has been set up ahead of time based on a curriculum developer's idea of who will be in the classroom" (p. 1211).

Multimedia learning curricula are decidedly different than more traditional text-based curricula. Integrating multimedia into the curriculum requires an understanding of cognition on the part of the preservice teacher student in relation to cognition of learners they will engage in school classrooms. Learners introduced to curriculum in integrated information (text in close proximity to visual media) with text in sequential order to visual lends itself to a more effective learning experience (Chandler & Sweller, 1991; Mayer, 2005a, 2009, 2010; Mayer & Sims, 1994). Integrated formats (e.g., presenting text and visual information in sequence on a single screen) are preferable to separate media (e.g., presenting information on screen and on a separate printed sheet).

Multimedia learning experiences are most effective when the content and format actively engage the learner. The participatory and active engagement helps the learner construct knowledge and organize information into meaningful schema (Mayer, 2003). Research tells us several ways in which we can make multimedia presentations more engaging (Mayer, 2005c).

Mayer (2005a) has noted that multimedia curriculum that is more personalized to the learner's needs creates a more authentic learning experience than multimedia curriculum that is less personalized. Presentations that have a more conversational tone tend to be more engaging than those that have a more formal tone (Mayer, 2005c).

Participatory Considerations

The "social" element of multimedia learning presents opportunity to enhance and increase the quality and quantity of social interactions that students have with their teachers, and vice versa, by overcoming the barriers of time and location (Jonassen, Lee, Yang, & Laffey, 2005). Integral to social interaction is an understanding that social media offer the neomillennial generation the ability to connect, interact, and share ideas in new and complementary ways. Teachers entering classrooms today often are confronted with the remnants of old ideological and technological foundations that do not support a sense of social interface commensurate with the experiences of neomillennial youth who have grown up with social media environments. Simply stated, as teacher educators preparing teachers for a Web 2.0 world, we are dealing with "a new sense of spatiality that defies the sorts of modernist understandings of knowledge, of place, of sociality that is [sic] so foundational to our own schooling experience and the normative social science and teacher training most of us underwent at some time in the last several decades" (Luke, 2006, p. 272).

Teacher educators will need first to examine their own beliefs and understandings with respect to technologies and media, then engage in transforming these beliefs and understandings into patterns of pedagogical practice and curricular design that provide multimedia and digital technology-enriched learning experiences for their students. Using digital technologies, such as social media, to cultivate engagement between the teacher educator and his preservice students is a critical center to creating participatory cultures of learning. Equally important is the integration of multimedia in curricula and instruction to enrich the learning opportunities and experiences in classrooms. Digital technologies and multimedia can, if embraced in a positive and meaningful manner, enhance the nature and quality of student-student interactions. Likewise, they can enhance the nature and quality of student-teacher interactions. Student engagement is enhanced when students have the opportunity to work with their peers, share ideas and resources, and reflect on the different perspectives their fellow students bring to class. Teacher educator and preservice student engagement is enhanced through social media when students are provided an opportunity to engage with teacher educators through cultures that have low barriers to social interaction, discussion, and creativity. The participatory culture enhanced via social media completes the learning-to-teach experience by overcoming barriers of time and location, as well as valuing students as authentic participants in the learning-to-teach experience.

These participatory cultures of learning are best advantaged by integrating multimedia as a spatial context for discourse, creativity, and deliberation in the process of learning to teach. In turn, the preservice teacher who experiences an authentic participatory learning culture in preparing to teach will take the experience forward into her teaching practice.

Spatial Considerations

The spatial nature of and access to knowledge are shifting dramatically. Only a few decades ago, preparing teachers for schools traditionally focused on "the culture of the book, monologic literacy, specialists in one disciplinary content area," with teachers "struggling with the new technologies" (Luke, 2006, p. 271). Spatial qualities of teaching and learning were defined, in large part, by the classroom and/or clinical site and the learning activities therein. Today, the spatial qualities of learning and knowledge are dramatically different, and "Web 2.0 tools offer a fundamental reorientation in educational technology" (Bartow, 2014, p. 40), adding a digital orientation to spatialization of teaching and learning.

Education is being redefined by advancement of social media. Society in general and educators in particular are challenged with a "new sense of spatiality that defies the sorts of modernist understandings of knowledge, of place, of sociality that is so foundational to our own schooling experience and the normative social science and teacher training most of us underwent at some time in the last several decades" (Luke, 2006, p. 272). Multimedia are integral to the lives of neomillennial youth and are redefining many aspects of daily life including how we communicate, learn, create, and consume knowledge (Leu, et al., 2009). The more traditional spatial nature of teaching and learning is now challenged by myriad alternative formal and informal learning opportunities centered on online platforms, networks, and communities that provide resource-enriched learning and options for more diverse topics and applications of knowledge in varied social contexts.

Teacher educators today are challenged to examine the implications of multimedia and digital technologies in creating new spatial considerations for learning and teaching, both in the preparation to teach and in the actual teaching for which preservice students are being prepared. The important caveat here is that how teacher educators learned to teach is no longer a viable option for preparing teachers who will be paired with neomillennial youth in today's schools. And the spatial nature of schools and classrooms has changed dramatically, often leaving teacher educators out of sync with the spatial needs of neomillennial youth and the teacher entering schools for the first time in a neomillennial era.

Whereas in past decades teaching and learning were limited to physical spaces of classrooms and clinical sites, multimedia and digital technologies challenge conventional paradigms and open media and digital technology doors, creating spatial qualities of learning heretofore unexperienced in teacher preparation and practice. Rethinking the spatial nature of and access to knowledge via social media recognizes that neomillennial youth as learners require different contexts and spaces for learning and that social media as spatialization of knowledge sharing presents a "starting point as learners increasingly tailor their personal needs and circumstances" (Bartow, 2014, p. 39). For the preservice student, experiencing social-mediated learning creates an awareness of and expertise in using social media as a means to generate discourse, construct knowledge, and value human capital, diminishing a cross-generational divide between teachers and students.

CONCLUSIONS

Integrating multimedia learning theory and digital technologies into teaching and learning can be both challenging and problematic if approached incorrectly or with indifference. Our responsibility, as teacher educators, is to engage our preservice students in learning experiences that prepare them for the reality of neomillennial youth today and the classrooms and schools they will enter as teachers. The neomillennial generation is increasingly more experienced in social media and other digital technologies, and it is a generation for which we must prepare teachers to communicate and interact in ways that do not default to learning that disengages or disenfranchises students. Although cautions are raised concerning use of new technologies, it is important to give consideration to multimedia learning in rethinking teacher preparation. The interactive nature of Web 2.0 media and digital technologies allows learners, preservice students preparing to teach and neomillennial youth entering pre-K–12 schools alike, to become authentic, active participants who co-construct the learning experience with their peers and teacher as they share and reflect on their individual interpretations and experiences to create a viable educational future.

Multimedia and digital technologies in the Web 2.0 world require a fundamental reorientation in educational technologies and learning theories as an infrastructure in teacher preparation. Myriad alternative formal and informal considerations for learning created by multimedia and digital technologies, Web 2.0 networks, in turn provide an enrichment of participatory cultures in educational settings—multimedia and digital technology-enriched communities—to learn about diverse topics and to apply knowledge in social contexts (Ala-Mutka, 2010). The task before us as teacher educators is to examine a world being redefined by Web 2.0 and situate teacher preparation appropriately in that world. Then we can begin the work of rethinking teacher preparation through the integration of multimedia learning.

Teacher preparation programs must reflect a new spatial diversity in teaching and learning, rebuilt and redesigned figuratively and literally through the seamless articulation of social media in how students of teaching are prepared and how teacher educators go about the preparation. Teacher preparation programs must be icons of new policy, new modalities of learning, new vistas of technological interface with schools and society (Ball, 2007). Teacher preparation needs to embrace new kinds of social and technological ecologies, new theories of learning such as multimedia learning. The risk, if we do not take this path, is the abandonment of neomillennial youth and the consequential furthering not only of the digital divide, but also an ideological and technology divide in the very foundation of our society and its educational systems.

NOTES

1. Mayer (2005a) defined "multimedia" as "presenting both words (such as spoken text or printed text) and pictures (such as illustrations, photos, animation, or video). By words, I mean that the material is presented in *verbal form*, such as using printed

text or spoken text. By pictures, I mean that the material is presented in *pictorial form*, such as using static graphics, including illustrations, graphs, diagrams, maps, or photos, or using dynamic graphics, including animation or video" (p. 2).

Multimedia learning, Mayer (2005a) explains, "occurs when people build mental representations from words (such as spoken text or printed text) and pictures (such as illustrations, photos, animation, or video) . . . *multimedia* refers to the presentation of words and pictures, whereas *learning* refers to the learner's construction of knowledge. The process by which people build mental representations from words and pictures is the focus of . . . cognitive theory of multimedia learning" (p. 2).

Mayer (2005a) further explains that five forms of representation of words and pictures occur as information is processed by memory. Each form represents a particular stage of processing in the three-memory stores model of multimedia learning. The first form of representation is the words and pictures in the multimedia presentation itself. The second form is the acoustic representation (sounds) and iconic representation (images) in sensory memory. The third form is the sounds and images in working memory. The fourth form of representation is the verbal and pictorial models that are also found in working memory. The fifth form is prior knowledge, or *schemas*, which are stored in long-term memory.

2. The term "Web 2.0" emerged in 2004, becoming a popular characterization of websites that allowed users to interact with each other as contributors to a website's content (see Rutherford, 2010). The features of Web 2.0 facilitate user engagement, collaboration, and interactive information sharing were a significant departure from traditional websites that were limited to the passive viewing of information (McLoughlin & Lee, 2007). The Web 2.0 moniker has now been applied to an expansive array of social media websites that rely heavily on the active engagement of their users to create, manipulate, and share content.

3. The term "digital divide," as used here, refers to various gaps between groups of people in their experiences with digital technologies (Haythornthwaite & Kendall, 2010).

4. The term "neomillennial" as used in this chapter connotes the "new" millennial generation. The neomillennial generation of today's society embodies a youth and culture wherein "mediated immersion" via social media technologies is increasingly the norm rather than the exception. Social interaction and learning are mediated via social media platforms. In this sense, engagement involves fluency in media and virtual settings, collaborative and communal learning, associational webs of representation, and learning experiences that address individual needs with low barriers to engagement and participation (see Bennett, Maton, & Kervin, 2008; Carlson, 2005; Dede, 2005a, 2005b; Dimock, 2018; Ferrarini & Mateer, 2014; Gardner & Eng, 2005; Howe & Strauss, 2000; Laughlin, Roper, & Howell, 2007; Oblinger, 2003; Prensky, 2001; Tapscott, 2009; Taylor, 2010).

5. Multi-spatial, for purposes of this discussion, connotes that Web 2.0 offers multiple social media spaces that allow the user to interface through social media tools and technologies. The neomillennial in today's society frequents multiple social media sites and uses multiple social media or digital technologies to engage in ways that redefine the nature of social interaction, conversation, community, and identity.

6. Mayer (2011) explains that research in the field of cognitive science "has identified five kinds of knowledge: facts—factual knowledge about the world; concepts—categories, schemas, models, or principles; procedures—step-by-step processes; strategies—general approaches; and beliefs—thoughts about learning" (Anderson et al., 2001; Mayer, 2010) (p. 6).

7. Mayer (2003) defines multimedia instructional message as a presentation consisting of words and pictures that is designed to foster meaningful learning. Thus, the definition has two parts: the presentation contains words and pictures, and it is designed to foster meaningful learning (p. 28).

8. Mayer (2003) explains that the "visualizer–verbalizer hypothesis is particularly relevant to the design of multimedia training because multimedia training involves presenting words and pictures to learners, but our interest also goes beyond multimedia training scenarios to understanding the cognitive style construct in general" (p. 833).

Verbalization and visualization as used in this chapter speak to how different forms of text- or verbal-based curriculum and visual-based curriculum are prepared and aligned as sequential knowledge for multimedia-based instruction messaging (Mayer, 2005a) in the delivery of the curriculum to the learner. The importance of the sequential delivery of verbal and visual forms of expression lies in the service of promoting student understanding.

REFERENCES

Ala-Mutka, K. (2010). *Learning in informal online networks and communities*. Joint Research Center Institute for Prospective Technological Studies. Accessed September 5, 2014, from http://ipts.jrc.ec.europa.eu/publications/pub.cfm?id=3059.

Anderson, L. W., Krathwohl, D. R., Airasian, P. W., Cruikshank, K. A., Mayer, R. E., Pintrich, P. R., Raths, J., & Wittrock, M. C. (2001). *A taxonomy of learning for teaching: A revision of Bloom's taxonomy of educational objectives*. New York, NY: Longman.

Baird, D. E., & Fisher, M. (2006). Neomillennial user experience design strategies: Utilizing social networking media to support "Always On" learning. *Journal of Educational Technology Systems, 34*(1), 5–32.

Ball, S. (2007). *Education plc: Understanding private sector participation in public sector education*. London: Routledge.

Barnes, K., Marateo, R., & Ferris, S. (2007). Teaching and learning with the net generation. *Innovate, 3*(4). http://www.innovateonline.info/index.php?view=article&id=382.

Bartow, S. M. (2014). Teaching with social media: Disrupting present day public education. *Educational Studies, 50*, 36–64.

Bennett, S., Maton, K., & Kervin, L. (2008). The "digital natives" debate: A critical review of the evidence. *British Journal of Educational Technology, 39*(5), 775–786. doi:10.1111/j.1467-8535.2007.00793.x.

Bigum, C., & Rowan, L. (2008). Landscaping on shifting ground: Teacher education in a digitally transformed world. *Asia-Pacific Journal of Teacher Education, 36*(3), 245–255.

Buckingham, D. (2003). *Media education: Literacy, learning and contemporary culture.* Cambridge: Polity Press.

Buckingham, D. (2007). *Schooling the digital generation: Popular culture, new media and the future of education.* London, UK: UCL IOE Press.

Buckingham, D., et al. (2005). *The media literacy of children and young people: A review of the academic research.* London, UK: Ofcom.

Carlson, S. (2005, October 7). The net generation goes to college. *Chronicle of Higher Education, 52*(7), A34.

Chandler, P., & Sweller, J. (1991). Cognitive load theory and the format of instruction. *Cognition and Instruction, 8,* 293–332.

Collins, A., & Halverson, R. (2009). *Rethinking education in the age of technology: The digital revolution and schooling in America.* New York, NY: Teachers College Press.

Cope, B., & Kalantzis, M. (2009). A grammar of multimodality. *International Journal of Learning. 16,* 361–425. doi: 10.1080/15544800903076044.

Dede, C. (2005a). Planning for neomillennial learning styles. *Educause Quarterly, 28*(1), 7–12.

Dede, C. (2005b). Planning for neomillennial learning styles: Implications for investments in technology and faculty. In D. G. Oblinger & J. L. Oblinger (Eds.), *Educating the net generations* (pp. 15.1–15.22). Louisville, CO: Educause. Retrieved September 9, 2014, from https://net.educause.edu/ir/library/pdf/pub7101o.pdf.

Depietro, P. (2013). *Transforming education with new media: Participatory pedagogy, interactive learning, and Web 2.0.* New York, NY: Peter Lang.

Dimock, M. (2018). Defining generations: Where millennials end and post-millennials begin. *Pew Research Center.* Retrieved from http://www.pewresearch.org/fact-tank/2018/03/01/defining-generations-where-millennials-end-and-post-millennials-begin/.

Facer, K., & Selwyn, N. (2010). Towards a sociology of education and technology. In R. Brooks, M. McCormack, & K. Bhopal (Eds.), *Contemporary debates in the sociology of education* (pp. 218–235). New York, NY: Palgrave Macmillan.

Ferrarini, T. H., & Mateer, G. D. (2014). Multimedia technology for the next generation. *Journal of Private Enterprise, 29*(2), 129–139.

Gardner, S., & Eng, S. (2005). What students want: Generation Y and the changing function of the academic library. *Libraries and the Academy, 5*(3), 405–420.

Gilakjani, A. P. (2012). A study on the impact of using multimedia to improve the quality of English language teacher. *Journal of Language Teaching and Research, 3*(6), 1208–1215.

Haythornthwaite, C., & Kendall, L. (2010). Internet and community. *American Behavioral Scientist, 53*(8), 1083–094.

Howe, N., & Strauss, B. (2000). *Millennials rising: The next great generation.* New York, NY: Vintage Books.

Ito, M., Horst, H., Bittanti, M., Boyd, D., Herr-Stephenson, B., Lange, P. B., Pascoe, C. J., & Robinson, L. (2008). *Living and learning with new media: Summary of findings from the Digital Youth Project.* Accessed September 10, 2014, at http://digitalyouth.ischool.berkeley.edu/files/report/digitalyouth-WhitePaper.pdf.

Jenkins, H., Clinton, K., Purushotma, R., Robison, A. J., & Weigel, M. (2009). Confronting the challenges of participatory media: Media education for the 21st century. Cambridge, MA: MIT Press. Accessed at https://mitpress.mit.edu/.../9780262513623_Confronting_the_Challenges.pdf.

Jonassen, D., Lee, C. B., Yang, C. C., & Laffey, J. (2005). The collaborative principle in multimedia learning. In R. E. Mayer (Ed.), *The Cambridge handbook of multimedia learning* (pp. 247–270). Cambridge, UK: Cambridge University Press.

Kaplan, A. M., & Haenlein, M. (2010). Users of the world, unite! The challenges and opportunities of social media. *Business Horizons, 53*(1), 59–68.

Kress, G. (2003). *Literacy in the new media age.* London, UK: Routledge.

Lambert, J., & Cuper, P. (2008). Multimedia technologies and familiar spaces: 21st-century teaching for 21st-century learners. *Contemporary Issues in Technology and Teacher Education, 8*(3), 264–276.

Lankshear, C., & Knobel, M. (2006). *New literacies: Everyday practices and classroom learning.* Maidenhead, UK: McGraw Hill/Open University Press.

Lankshear, C., & Knobel, M. (Eds.). (2008). *Digital literacies: Concepts, policies and practices.* New York, NY: Peter Lang.

Laughlin, D., Roper, M., & Howell, K. (2007). NASA eEducation roadmap: Research challenges in the design of massively multiplayer games for education & training. Retrieved September 10, 2014, from http://www.fas.org/programs/ltp/policy_and_publications/routmaps/_docs/NASA%20eEduction%20Roadmap.pdf.

Leu, D., O'Byrne, W. I., Zawilinski, L., McVerry, J. G., & Everett-Cacopard, H. (2009). Comments on Greenho, Robelia, and Hughes: Expanding the new literacies conversation. *Educational Researcher, 38*(4), 264–269.

Lotherington, H., & Jenson, J. (2011). Teaching multimodal and digital literacy in L2 settings: New literacies, new basics, new pedagogies. *Annual Review of Applied Linguistics, 31,* 226–246.

Luke, C. (2006). Cyberpedagogy. In J. Weiss, J. Nolan, J. Hunsinger, & P. Trifonas (Eds.), *The international handbook of virtual learning environments* (pp. 269–277). Dordrecht, The Netherlands: Springer.

Mayer, R. E. (2003). The promise of multimedia learning: Using the same instructional design methods across different media. *Learning and Instruction, 12,* 125–139.

Mayer, R. E. (2004a). Teaching of subject matter. In S. T. Fiske (Ed.), *Annual Review of Psychology* (Vol. 55, pp. 715–744). Palo Alto, CA: Annual Reviews.

Mayer, R. E. (2004b). Should there be a three strikes rule against pure discovery? The case for guided methods of instruction. *American Psychologist, 59*(1), 14–19.

Mayer, R. E. (2005a). Introduction to multimedia learning. In R. E. Mayer (Ed.), *The Cambridge handbook of multimedia learning* (pp. 1–18). Cambridge, UK: Cambridge University Press.

Mayer, R. E. (2005b). Cognitive theory of multimedia learning. In R. E. Mayer (Ed.), *The Cambridge handbook of multimedia learning* (pp. 31–48). Cambridge, UK: Cambridge University Press.

Mayer, R. E. (2005c). Principles of multimedia learning based on social cues: Personalization, voice, and image principles. In R. E. Mayer (Ed.), *The Cambridge handbook of multimedia learning* (pp. 201–214). Cambridge, UK: Cambridge University Press.

Mayer, R. E. (2008). *Learning and instruction* (2nd ed.). Upper Saddle River, NJ: Pearson Merrill Prentice Hall.

Mayer, R. E. (2009). *Multimedia learning* (2nd ed.). New York, NY: Cambridge University Press.

Mayer, R. E. (2010). *Applying the science of learning.* Upper Saddle River, NJ: Pearson.

Mayer, R. E. (2011, January 16). *Applying the science of learning to undergraduate science education.* Paper commissioned for the Committee on the Status, Contributions, and Future Directions of Discipline Based Education Research. Washington, DC: National Academies Board of Science Education.

Mayer, R. E., & Massa, L. J. (2003). Three facets of visual and verbal learners: Cognitive ability, cognitive style, and learning preference. *Journal of Educational Psychology, 4*, 833–846. doi:10.1037/0022-0663.95.4.833.

Mayer, R. E., & Sims, V. K. (1994). For whom is a picture worth a thousand words? Extensions of a dual-coding theory of multimedia learning. *Journal of Educational Psychology, 86*, 389–401.

Moran, M., Seaman, J., & Tinti-Kane, H. (2011). *Teaching, learning, and sharing: How today's higher education faculty use social media.* New York, NY: Pearson Learning Solutions.

Oblinger, D. (2003). Boomers, Gen-Zers, and Millennials: Understanding the "new students." *EDUCAUSE Review, 38*(4), 37–47.

Prenksy, M. (2001). Digital natives, digital immigrants. *On the Horizon, 9,* 5, 1–6.

Rutherford, C. (2010). Using online social media to support preservice student engagement. *MERLOT Journal of Online Learning and Teaching, 6*(4), 703–711.

Saltmarsh, S., & Sunderland-Smith, W. (2010). S(t)imulating learning: Pedagogy, subjectivity and teacher education in online environments. *London Review of Education, 8,* 15–24.

Selwyn, N. (2011). *Schools and schooling in the digital age: A critical analysis.* New York, NY: Routledge.

Shih, W., & Allen, M. (2006). Working with Generation-D: Adopting and adapting to cultural learning and change. *Library Management, 28*(1/2), 89–100.

Shirky, C. (2008). *Here comes everybody: The power of organising without organisations.* London, UK: Allen Lane.

Tapscott, D. (2009). *Grown up digital: The rise of the net generation.* New York, NY: McGraw-Hill.

Taylor, (2010). Teaching Generation NeXt: A pedagogy for today's learners. In *A collection of papers on self-study and institutional improvement* (26th ed., pp. 192–196). Chicago, IL: Higher Learning Commission.

Chapter 9

Multimedia Learning and the Educational Leader

Scott McLeod

INTRODUCTION

Whether we are watching or making learning videos, using interactive maps and diagrams on our iPads, connecting with other classrooms across the globe via videoconferencing or blogging, recording screencasts to help improve the knowledge of peers, or engaging in a variety of other learning and teaching tasks, it is clear that the historical dominance of printed text on paper is waning and that multimedia tools and environments are suffusing how we learn (Bonk, 2009). As the internet and other digital technologies rapidly and radically transform our information and learning landscapes, school leaders, their staffs, and the communities they serve all must adapt if they wish to be relevant to the new digital, global world that we all now inhabit.

As the other chapters in this book illustrate quite clearly, technology tools and multimedia are increasingly important components of student and educator learning, both formal and informal. This chapter will examine the role of the educational leader in multimedia learning environments.

SHIFT IN MEDIA AND DIGITAL TECHNOLOGIES

Shifts from analog to digital—and from local to global—present significant challenges to our schools. Our educational systems were designed for a different era, one in which most graduates went on to do manual labor in the agricultural or manufacturing sectors and only a few elite students went on to higher education or professional careers (Collins & Halverson, 2009). Today, the demands of modern-day digital citizenship and our new hyper-connected, hypercompetitive global information society require a reversal of schools' traditional preparation.

On the economic front, most employees, at least in developed nations, now are knowledge workers who primarily use their heads and their hearts rather than their bodies (Levy & Murnane, 2004). It is extremely difficult to find a well-paying job in a modern, creative economy that doesn't require heavy usage of digital technologies.

If the industrial revolution was about augmenting and replacing our physical labor with machines, the information revolution is about enhancing and substituting our mental labor with computers (Brynjolfsson & McAfee, 2011). On the citizenship front, consuming a small handful of broadcast channels (i.e., newspapers, radio, television, and magazines) is no longer sufficient.

Today, we must juggle dozens, if not hundreds, of competing information channels, viewpoints, and media sources in order to make informed political decisions (Sunstein, 2009). Whether for professional purposes, personal learning and growth, or participation in complex digital political environments, it is clear that the skill sets for life success are changing rapidly.

Implementing digital change within outdated analog school systems is an extraordinarily complex task. Internal cultures and lack of support structures often mitigate against effective adoption of digital technologies. So too do external funding streams, policy environments, and community belief systems. Nonetheless, school principals and superintendents must figure out ways to create, facilitate, and maintain student learning environments that are both more cognitively complex and more technology-suffused. To do otherwise is a disservice to our current and future graduates.

WHAT DOES EFFECTIVE MULTIMEDIA LEADERSHIP LOOK LIKE?

Given the demands of school and society, one might hope for a robust—or at least rapidly emerging—research base related to the leadership of multimedia learning and schooling. Unfortunately, that is not the case. Technology-related articles in peer-reviewed educational leadership journals are few and far between. Educational administration dissertations and education research conference presentations also are scarce when it comes to addressing technology leadership issues in P–12 schools (McLeod & Richardson, 2011). As such, the research literature tells us very little about what it means to be an effective leader of multimedia learning environments.

Currently, the best framework we have for effective technology leadership is the set of *National Educational Technology Standards for Administra-*

tors (NETS-A) from the International Society for Technology in Education (ISTE, 2009b). Although the standards are not explicitly based on research, they were created using national consensus-building techniques and generally have been accepted as the dominant model for thinking about the leadership side of multimedia learning and teaching. Now in their second iteration, the NETS-A contain five primary standards:

1. visionary leadership
2. digital-age learning culture
3. excellence in professional practice
4. systemic improvement
5. digital citizenship

Each standard contains three to five performance indicators that further elucidate what administrators would do to satisfy the standard. Example performance indicators include: "*2b. Provide learner-centered environments equipped with technology and learning resources to meet the individual, diverse needs of all learners*"; "*3c. Promote and model effective communication and collaboration among stakeholders using digital age tools*" and; "*5b. Promote, model and establish policies for safe, legal, and ethical use of digital information and technology.*" Although more detailed than the five standards, the twenty-one performance indicators in the NETS-A are still fairly broad and vague. In the sections that follow, each standard is explicated in more detail in order to provide a more concrete description of effective leadership of multimedia learning and teaching.

VISIONARY LEADERSHIP

Facilitating organizational vision is one of the most critical roles of leaders. A vision for powerful technology integration and implementation in schools must necessarily begin with a deep understanding of the characteristics of our new technological environments. For example, in the future, our learning will be even more digital—and less analog—than it is now. It will be more online and also more mobile, available any time and anywhere from a multitude of internet-connected computing devices.

Our new information landscape is now incredibly networked and interconnected. It is increasingly open and free, and thus accessible in ways that costly print and/or electronically broadcast materials are not (Willinsky, 2006). Low barriers to entry online facilitate the participation of billions of individuals on both the content consumption and content creation sides of the equation, resulting in an often overwhelming blossoming of ideas and resources (Shirky, 2008). New techniques such as "crowdsourcing" and "crowdfunding" enable creation of learning content and tools that in the past were literally impossible to implement.

The development of online and/or software-mediated educational tools and environments is reducing our dependency on live human instructors and is opening up opportunities for millions of people whose learning needs previously went unmet (Christensen, Horn, & Johnson, 2008). Our learning resources increasingly are multimedia—incorporating text, images, audio, video, diagrams, charts, maps, simulations, and games—and often are much more interactive than previous generations of learning materials.

As a result of these shifts, we now have unprecedented power to access the world's body of information in ways previously unimaginable. Decreasing barriers to information access cause our learning to become more self-directed and thus more personalized. We also are seeing incredible growth in informal learning opportunities, many of which compete directly with formal learning institutions such as schools and universities.

Principals and superintendents must be able to communicate these shifts to students, staff, and parents in ways that are emotionally resonant and foster movement in necessary directions. Where a sense of urgency is lacking, administrators must create and sustain long-term change mind-sets. Successful leaders will be able to facilitate school organizations that recognize that digital technologies are important, that multimedia learning and teaching are here to stay, and that learning environments must be continually flexible and adaptable to new—and often frighteningly swift—changes in our information landscape.

Finally, in addition to the work that school leaders must do within their educational organizations, they also must be educators and advocates for both local and larger external communities. Not only must administrators bring parents and community members on board, but they also must successfully educate school board members and state and national policy makers. Numerous changes in local, state, and federal policies must be enacted in order productively to transition current schools into a digital, global era.

DIGITAL-AGE LEARNING CULTURE

In earlier decades, school administrators were viewed primarily as managers, responsible for ensuring that budgets, facilities, personnel, and other aspects of schooling ran smoothly. More recently, we have shifted to understanding that significant and long-lasting changes in classroom cultures and student outcomes are dependent on principals and superintendents also serving as leaders of learning and transformation, not just managers (see, e.g., Duke, 1987; Hallinger, 1992).

When it comes to digital technologies, facilitating effective learning integration is the most important—but also perhaps the most difficult—task that school leaders face. Like teachers, administrators often are unfamiliar with digital devices and environments. Even if they are users of digital technologies in their personal lives, school leaders may not adequately understand learning and/or teaching uses of those tools. Ramping up to technology-suffused pedagogy is necessary but also can be quite onerous.

Principals and superintendents need deep understandings of what effective technology integration looks like (Mishra & Koehler, 2006). It is not enough for administrators simply to place quantities of computers in schools and classrooms and then hope that teachers and students use them.

Leaders also must be able to discern the quality of technology usage in the instructional process. Otherwise, schools run the very real risk of using technology for technology's sake rather than for meaningful, relevant, and authentic learning purposes. Effective leaders of multimedia learning will institute models and frameworks, system-wide discussions, classroom observation and evaluation techniques, and other evaluative and nonevaluative mechanisms that facilitate explicit analysis and recognition of appropriate and powerful technology integration.

Some of the most significant barriers to teachers' effective usage of technology relate to the lack of systemic supports. Many of these are embodied in ISTE's *Essential Conditions* document (ISTE, 2009a), which outlines numerous factors that must be in place for effective technology integration to occur. One critical support condition is the presence of adequate technical support personnel. Schools usually burden information technology staff with far greater computer support ratios than do for-profit or other nonprofit organizations (McLeod, 2003).

Overburdened by the sheer numbers of hardware, software, and educators under their domain, school technology personnel often are unable to provide robust support for classroom technology integration. This frequently results in long waits for assistance and/or repairs, with concurrent impacts on teachers' willingness to implement digital technologies in their instruction. School systems also typically underinvest in technology integration personnel, using their monies instead for devices, software, and networks and the people to maintain them. Classroom teachers thus have nowhere to turn for integration assistance other than peers and the occasional professional development day.

In addition to ensuring better technical support structures, administrators also must work with teachers, curriculum developers, and subject-area experts to ensure that digital technologies are appropriately aligned with and operate in service of instructional and curricular goals (Jacobs, 2010). Too often technologies are purchased without appropriate understandings of how they will be used instructionally.

Tales are legion of computing technologies sitting unused throughout our nation's school systems (see Cuban, 2001). School leaders frequently are susceptible to vendors' sales pitches and should take great care to incorporate the input of end users into technology purchasing and decision-making processes. Administrators also must be aware of and mitigate against schools' general tendency to purchase teacher-centric technologies such as interactive whiteboards, document cameras, and student response systems rather than student-centric technologies such as laptops, tablet computers, digital cameras and camcorders, and scientific probeware for which students, not teachers, are the primary users.

Resources are always scarce, and funding streams are never enough. As such, school leaders should strive to get maximal outcomes from their technology investments. Although it is important for teachers to be effective users of digital technologies, it is even more critical that students graduate from our school systems as technology-fluent citizens, able to meet learning, citizenship, and workplace demands as needed (November, 2010; Trilling & Fadel, 2009). Schools do not achieve this goal by having students passively observe others using technology.

School leaders also must attend to so-called digital divide issues. Historical conceptions of the digital divide have related to inequitable access to computers and/or the internet by traditionally underserved student populations and their families. The access gap is steadily closing—both at school and at home—but there is growing recognition of a secondary divide related to usage.

As Neumann (1991) noted long ago, economically disadvantaged students often are relegated to using computers for more remedial and less interesting purposes than their more affluent student peers. Administrators should ensure that all students have frequent and regular opportunities to use digital learning technologies in ways that are cognitively and creatively robust.

EXCELLENCE IN PROFESSIONAL PRACTICE

When it comes to improving professional practice, school leaders must recognize that most classroom educators have a fairly steep learning curve when it comes to digital technologies. Administrators should provide appropriate opportunities for professional learning as well as rich, robust support structures for teachers and students.

All too often, however, teachers are given no learning support whatsoever or are subjected to a several-hour training session—with no later follow-up—that focuses on tool-specific functions rather than on how new digital learning technologies can support instructional and student learning goals. School systems for which this is an accurate description of technology-related professional development should be unsurprised to see few, if any, positive outcomes from their technology implementation efforts.

For effective integration to occur, teachers must steadily acquire new technology skills in the service of learning goals. Many schools have seen great success with interest-driven, teacher-led technology inquiry groups or learning communities in which educators work together to learn new technologies and ascertain their appropriateness and fit for students' learning (see Hughes, Kerr, & Ooms, 2005).

If schools are struggling to provide adequate access to dedicated technology integration personnel, the pairing of student technology "mentors" with adult educator "mentees" can help mitigate teachers' and administrators' technology-related learning needs (Harper, 2008). Another potential solution when full-time technology integration personnel are scarce is for school leaders to find ways to explicitly and structurally tap into the expertise and enthusiasm of early adopters who already work within the school or district.

Most technology-savvy teachers are more than happy to share their experiences and learning tools with faculty peers and would be delighted to have more formal structures in which to do so. For all of these initiatives, administrators must set aside dedicated time, structures, and other supports to ensure success.

When encouraging greater technology integration, school leaders must walk a fine line between maintaining a sense of urgency and giving staff sufficient time to be digital learners. Administrators also must be digital learners themselves. If they want staff to integrate learning technologies into their classrooms, they must model appropriate and powerful technology usage in their own roles.

This modeling must include explicit conversation around the need to set aside fear and egos in favor of a willingness to take risks and be learners. Leaders who visibly and transparently model the technology learning process—and the inevitable failure and relearning that occur—will see greater willingness by teachers to do the same.

One of the most difficult tasks for administrators and teachers is to stay abreast of new developments in educational technology. On the scholarly front, digital technologies are changing much faster than traditional research and publication structures can handle. It often takes several years for a study to be initiated, implemented, written, submitted, accepted, and published.

By the time a research article or evaluation report becomes available to the public, the technology of concern—and its essential functions and capabilities—may have morphed several generations or even disappeared altogether, replaced by something newer or better. Traditional publishing structures often are inadequate for addressing rapidly developing technologies (which may describe all learning technologies these days).

One possible solution to this lack of timeliness is for administrators to create—and to encourage their staff and students to create—so-called personal (or professional) learning networks (PLNs). General amalgamations of RSS readers, Twitter feeds, YouTube channel subscriptions, social bookmarking services, and other resource curation and sharing tools, PLNs stand for the idea that powerful personal and professional learning can occur in informal online spaces, not just in set-aside, district-provided professional development sessions.

Millions of students and educators around the world are using social media, content curation, and other technologies to connect and collaborate with role-alike peers, learn from and with subject-matter experts, and create and share resources (Nussbaum-Beach & Hall, 2011). The power of these informal learning networks, or PLNS, is illustrated by the near-evangelical enthusiasm of their participants. As such, PLNS may be one of a school organization's most-promising avenues for providing learning opportunities for staff and students.

Finally, one often-neglected area of technology usage by administrators is their own professional or organizational communication. A recent study (Cox, 2012) shows that some principals and superintendents are leveraging social media to great effect with both internal and external stakeholders.

Using tools such as blogs, Facebook, Twitter, and YouTube, administrators are beginning to understand that social media can help them connect with parents, community members, staff, and students in ways that are more immediate, more authentic, more visible, and more impactful than traditional means such as weekly flyers, static websites, email listservs, and the local cable television channel (Stock, 2009). School systems have a great deal to learn from corporations and nonprofits about how to use social media effectively and thoughtfully to accomplish organizational communication goals.

SYSTEMIC IMPROVEMENT

An important component of any multimedia learning initiative should be the identification of appropriate measures of success. School systems should monitor pertinent outcomes to ensure adequate return on their instructional, technological, and personnel capacity-building investments.

One challenge in this area is that digital technologies, future citizenry demands, and global workforce needs all are pushing toward more cognitively abstract student outcomes. When most graduates simply needed relatively basic knowledge and skills in order to join what were primarily manufacturing economies (Autor, Levy, & Murnane, 2003), student learning outcomes were measured fairly easily with crude letter grades, standardized tests, and in-class assessments of low-level cognitive work. As countries all over the world recognize that greater percentages of graduates need better mastery of higher-level cognitive work for both citizenship and workforce purposes, assessing student learning outcomes such as the ability effectively to analyze, communicate, create, collaborate, or innovate becomes much more difficult (Schraw & Robinson, 2011).

Many other nations are ahead of America when it comes to assessing higher-order thinking skills (Darling-Hammond, 2010). In the United States, two national consortia—the Partnership for Assessment of Readiness for College and Careers (2012) and the Smarter Balanced Assessment Consortium (2012)—are attempting to create computer-delivered assessments that address the nearly ubiquitous Common Core State Standards. The aim of both the standards and the assessments is to focus more on higher-level cognitive work by students.

The Council for Aid to Education (2012) has a similar goal and has created college- and work-readiness assessments that can be taken by secondary or postsecondary students. States such as New Hampshire and Maine are using senior projects, portfolios, and other assessments to move more toward performance-based assessment of graduates.

Likewise, several networks of charter schools—including the New Tech Network, Big Picture Learning, Envision, Expeditionary Learning, Band of Educators, Edvisions, and Independent Curriculum Group schools—are focusing on aspects of schooling such as greater facilitation of student inquiry, project- or problem-based learning, competency-based student progression, and alternative assessment of student mastery. School leaders who wish to move both student learning and assessment in more cognitively complex (and thus abstract) directions should connect with and learn from these pacesetters.

More informally, some schools are developing their own local rubrics for assessing higher-level thinking work, and many are finding that digital technologies provide myriad alternatives for students to display mastery of their learning. Schools with student laptop initiatives and other technology-rich schools increasingly are removing technical and policy barriers such as technology bans and overly restrictive internet filters, instead giving students fairly wide-ranging choice over the learning tools they use and how they demonstrate what they have learned. Although the research base in this area is fairly limited, what exists seems to complement a wealth of anecdotal evidence that students appear to be more engaged and interested in their learning activities when greater voice and agency are accompanied by access to powerful digital learning tools and environments (Sauers & McLeod, 2012).

One important role of principals and superintendents is ensuring that employee position announcements, job descriptions, hiring processes, mentoring systems, training, and evaluation criteria all enforce school organizations' need for robust multimedia learning and teaching. Few school systems currently have powerful technology integration as a core competency for classroom teaching staff. Educational organizations' omission of digital teaching proficiency and the ability to facilitate students' higher-order thinking as essential, required skill sets for teachers and administrators sends clear signals to current faculty, job candidates, and educator preparation programs about institutional values. Until this changes, meaningful and authentic uses of multimedia technologies in P–12 classrooms will continue to be isolated aberrations rather than routine observances.

Over the past several decades, school systems slowly have instituted a variety of technical systems to facilitate the management of lower-level cognitive work. Student information systems, online grade books, electronic formative assessment tools, and data warehouses all are examples of technologies that help educators input, manage, analyze, and present student learning data (Wayman, Stringfield, & Yakimowski, 2004). Most of the data in these institutional systems focus on student demographic information, letter grades, test scores, and daily assignment tracking.

As educational organizations transition to student learning environments that place greater emphasis on higher-order thinking skills, they will need more robust technology tools that allow them to facilitate, collect, and evaluate more complex, abstract, open-ended student learning. Most of these tools do not yet exist, so it is difficult to envision at this time what they might look like. They are likely to include evolving features such as sophisticated document and portfolio management (including archiving and tagging of multimedia student and teacher work products); deep cross-artifact text, image, audio, and video analysis; infographic-like presentation of underlying patterns and meaning; and the ability to easily but selectively share through a variety of information and social media channels.

Other tools to facilitate effective learning and teaching will include system-provided technologies such as open-access content repositories, streaming multimedia servers, online adaptive learning systems, and robust, social media-driven collaboration channels for students, classroom teachers, and administrators. Strategic partnerships with state and federal governments, corporations, foundations, nonprofits, and others will become more prevalent as school systems face inevitable gaps in funding and resources. Growth in these and other technology systems must be accompanied by concurrent growth in organizational thinking as well as administrative and societal permission and encouragement to use these tools.

DIGITAL CITIZENSHIP

In most school organizations, numerous policies, processes, and belief systems impede the effective use of multimedia technologies. For example, technology coordinators' desires to maintain the integrity of the computing systems for which they're responsible often directly conflict with educators' desires to enable learning resources for themselves and students.
Similarly, fearful parents, school boards, and community members can place enormous pressures on administrators to restrict student and teacher access to only a small handful of approved tools and websites. Digital devices and online environments are proliferating swiftly, and power is devolving from centralized institutions to individuals. Navigating the balance between enabling powerful learning and ensuring safe and appropriate use by students and educators has never been more difficult.

School administrators should begin with the end in mind: powerful, technology-suffused learning and teaching that focus on higher-order as well as lower-order thinking. To increase the prevalence of meaningful technology integration in school classrooms, principals and superintendents must work persistently to facilitate organizational mind-sets of enablement and empowerment rather than fear (McLeod, 2008).

Necessary strategies include age- and role-differentiated internet filtering and acceptable use policies; digital citizenship curricula for students of all ages; and open, honest stakeholder discussions that include students and focus on both positive and negative aspects of cultural transformations wrought by technology. Few administrators currently are fostering the types of conversations that their internal and external communities need to have in order to come to shared understandings about the role of digital technologies in learning, teaching, schooling, and society. Similarly, robust digital citizenship dialogues rarely occur in most educational organizations.

Proactive modeling and teaching of appropriate and powerful uses of technology help students acquire desired skills and belief systems much better than the typical combination of preaching, prohibiting, and otherwise leaving youth to fend for themselves (Richardson, 2010). School curricula that foster citizenship discussions should include sophisticated discussions around issues of intellectual property, copyright, openness and sharing, and the global information commons.

Internal policy review and revision are key to the success of school technology integration and implementation. Relevant school board policies—as well as local school rules and decision making—should be reexamined for inhibiting effects on student and teacher technology usage. Potential target policies might include those regarding student cell phone usage, internet filtering, acceptable student and employee use of computers, the ability of students to bring their own devices (BYOD), and employees' usage of social media and other electronic communication channels.

When formulating or revising policies, board members and administrators also should remember that they are sending messages about what their school organization values (Martinez, 2008). If school systems desire better integration of multimedia with student learning, policies and rhetoric must align with organizational goals.

CONCLUSION

Research has found quite consistently that school leadership is "second only to teaching among school-related factors in its impact on student learning" (Leithwood, Louis, Anderson, & Wahlstrom, 2004, p. 3). When we think about effective leadership of multimedia learning, we must start with the recognition that ultimately school administrators, not classroom educators, control all of the resources necessary for systemic change, including time, money, vision, personnel allocation, professional development, and internal policy. If the leaders don't get it, it doesn't happen.

Unfortunately, because of lack of knowledge, fear, philosophical concerns, generational differences, or other factors, right now most principals and superintendents are struggling when it comes to multimedia learning and teaching. As noted above, the job of facilitating effective technology usage by students and teachers is both complex and challenging. Our administrators need greater support and training than they currently are receiving.

Principals and superintendents who wish to facilitate technology-rich learning environments have few places to turn, however. Few university educational leadership preparation programs have the faculty expertise or the coursework to train technology-savvy administrators (McLeod, Bathon, & Richardson, 2011). Here in the United States, school districts, state and national educational leadership associations, and state departments of education aren't doing much beyond an occasional training day or conference session (McLeod, 2011).

Most states have an annual educational technology conference, but those sessions typically focus on classroom teachers, media specialists, and technology coordinators; only a few states have dedicated technology strands or conferences for administrators. Corporate and foundation funding aimed at school technology initiatives almost invariably is aimed at students and teachers rather than at administrators. In short, the learning and support landscape for school technology leaders is pretty barren, littered with sporadic training sessions that lack both coherence and long-term commitment. If we wish to see systemic improvements in multimedia learning, teaching, and schooling, we must do better by our administrators.

REFERENCES

Autor, D. H., Levy, F., & Murnane, R. J. (2003). The skill content of recent technological change: An empirical exploration. *Quarterly Journal of Economics, 118*(4), 1279–1333.

Bonk, C. J. (2009). *The world is open: How web technology is revolutionizing education.* San Francisco, CA: Jossey-Bass.

Brynjolfsson, E., & McAfee, A. (2011). *Race against the machine: How the digital revolution is accelerating innovation, driving productivity, and irreversibly transforming employment and the economy.* Lexington, MA: Digital Frontier Press.

Christensen, C. M., Horn, M. B., & Johnson, C. W. (2008). *Disrupting class: How disruptive innovation will change the way the world learns.* New York, NY: McGraw-Hill.

Collins, A., & Halverson, R. (2009). *Rethinking education in the age of technology: The digital revolution and schooling in America.* New York, NY: Teachers College Press.

Council for Aid to Education. (2012). *About CAE.* Retrieved from http://www.cae.org/content/about.htm.

Cox, D. D. (2012). *School communications 2.0: A social media strategy for K–12 principals and superintendents* (unpublished doctoral dissertation). Iowa State University, Ames, IA.

Cuban, L. (2001). *Oversold and underused: Computers in the classroom.* Cambridge, MA: Harvard University Press.

Darling-Hammond, L. (2010). *The flat world and education: How America's commitment to equity will determine our future.* New York, NY: Teachers College Press.

Duke, D. L. (1987). *School leadership and instructional improvement.* New York, NY: Random House.

Hallinger, P. (1992). The evolving role of American principals: From managerial to instructional to transformational leaders. *Journal of Educational Administration, 30*(3), 35–48.

Harper, D. (2008). *Vision to action: Adding student leadership to your technology plan.* Olympia, WA: Generation Yes.

Hughes, J. E., Kerr, S., & Ooms, A. (2005). Content-focused technology inquiry groups: Cases of situated teacher learning and technology integration. *Journal of Educational Computing Research, 32*(4), 367–380.

International Society for Technology in Education (ISTE). (2009a). *Essential conditions*. Eugene, OR: Author.

International Society for Technology in Education (ISTE). (2009b). *National educational technology standards for administrators*. Eugene, OR: Author.

Jacobs, H. H. (2010). *Curriculum 21: Essential education for a changing world*. Alexandria, VA: ASCD.

Leithwood, K., Louis, K. S., Anderson, S., & Wahlstrom, K. (2004). *How leadership influences student learning*. New York, NY: Wallace Foundation.

Levy, F., & Murnane, R. (2004). *The new division of labor: How computers are creating the next job market*. Princeton, NJ: Princeton University Press.

Martinez, S. (2008). *What message does your AUP send home?* Retrieved from http://blog.genyes.org/index.php/2008/05/08/what-message-does-your-aup-send-home.

McLeod, S. (2003). *National district technology coordinators study. Technical report 1: Personal and professional characteristics*. Naperville, IL: North Central Regional Educational Laboratory, United States Department of Education.

McLeod, S. (2008, May). Blocking the future. *School Administrator, 65*(5), 8.

McLeod, S. (2011). Are we irrelevant to the digital, global world in which we now live? *UCEA Review, 52*(2), 1–5.

McLeod, S., Bathon, J. M., & Richardson, J. W. (2011). Studies of technology tool usage are not enough. *Journal of Research in Leadership Education, 6*(5), 288–297.

McLeod, S., & Richardson, J. W. (2011). The dearth of technology-related articles in educational leadership scholarship. *Journal of School Leadership, 21*(2), 216–240.

Mishra, P., & Koehler, M. J. (2006). Technological pedagogical content knowledge: A framework for integrating technology in teacher knowledge. *Teachers College Record, 108*(6), 1017–1054.

Neumann, D. (1991). *Technology and equity*. Syracuse, NY: ERIC Clearinghouse on Information Resources. (ERIC Document Reproduction Service No. ED 339400).

November, A. (2010). Technology rich, information poor. In J. Bellanca & R. Brandt (Eds.), *21st century skills: Rethinking how students learn* (pp. 275–284). Bloomington, IN: Solution Tree.

Nussbaum-Beach, S., & Hall, L. R. (2011). *The connected educator: Learning and leading in a digital age*. Bloomington, IN: Solution Tree.

Partnership for Assessment of Readiness for College and Careers (PARCC). (2012). *About PARCC*. Retrieved from http://www.parcconline.org/about-parcc.

Richardson, W. (2010). Navigating social networks as learning tools. In J. Bellanca & R. Brandt (Eds.), *21st century skills: Rethinking how students learn* (pp. 285–304). Bloomington, IN: Solution Tree.

Sauers, N. J., & McLeod, S. (2012, May). *What does the research say about school one-to-one computing initiatives?* [research brief]. Lexington, KY: UCEA Center for the Advanced Study of Technology Leadership in Education.

Schraw, G., & Robinson, D. R. (Eds.). (2011). *Assessment of higher order thinking skills*. Charlotte, NC: Information Age Publishing.

Shirky, C. (2008). *Here comes everybody: The power of organizing without organizations.* New York, NY: Penguin Press.

Smarter Balanced Assessment Consortium (SBAC). (2012). *About SBAC.* Retrieved from http://www.smarterbalanced.org/about.

Stock, M. J. (2009). *The school administrator's guide to blogging: A new way to connect with the community.* Lanham, MD: Rowman & Littlefield.

Sunstein, C. R. R. (2009). *Republic.com 2.0.* Princeton, NJ: Princeton University Press.

Trilling, B., & Fadel, C. (2009). *21st century skills: Learning for life in our times.* San Francisco, CA: Jossey-Bass.

Wayman, J. C., Stringfield, S., & Yakimowski, M. (2004). Software enabling school improvement through analysis of student data (CRESPAR Technical Report No. 67). Baltimore, MD: Johns Hopkins University.

Willinsky, J. (2006). *The access principle: The case for open access to research and scholarship.* Cambridge, MA: MIT Press.

Chapter 10

Epilogue

The Future of Multimedia Learning in Education

Patrick M. Jenlink

INTRODUCTION

What the future holds for education, in particular for teaching and learning, as a response to multimedia learning[1] and digital technologies and a new generation of learner already digitally literate is yet to be determined. However, preparing for that future requires that we as educators consider the challenges ahead.

Venturing into the frontier of a technologically driven future will require that educators understand the digital wave that has created a virtual digital architecture for socialization, communication, and learning. That said, no generation is more at ease with media and digital technologies than today's youth entering public schools and universities, a generation that has grown up in a multimedia- and technology-enriched environment.

THE CURRENT GENERATION

The current generation is demonstrating the impact of having been born and growing up in a world increasingly defined by digital technologies and media. As Green and Hannon (2007) note, these youth have been completely normalized by digital technologies; it is a fully integrated aspect of their lives and how they experience life. Many students in this group are using new media and technologies that did not exist for their parents "to *create* new things in new ways, *learn* new things in new ways, and *communicate* in new ways with new people—behaviors that have become hardwired in their ways of thinking and operating in the world" (Klopfer, Osterwell, Groff, & Haas, 2009, pp. 1–2).

The challenges of teaching and learning in a media- and digital technologies-enriched world pinpoint the need for new theories of learning, new understanding of cognition, new ways of communicating information, new ways of instructional design,[2] and new ways of teaching a digital generation that is well advanced in the use of digital technologies. Marshall McLuhan (1964) was instructive when he stated, "the personal and social consequences of any medium—that is, of any extension of ourselves—result from the new scale that is introduced into our affairs by each extension of ourselves, or by any new technology" (p. 9).

Media and digital technologies are necessary to teaching a digital generation[3] of learners already normalized to them. Multimedia learning theory and cognitive load theory are necessary to understand and engage in new ways of teaching, using new instructional strategies in the classroom.

Multimedia learning theory and digital technologies offer important consideration for bringing a change of emphasis in teaching from teacher-directed or teacher-centered learning to learner-centered and interactive learning. Multimedia integrated instruction offers an alternative to the current learning processes characteristic of more traditional classrooms. Multimedia learning theory informs teachers' understanding of the interface between teacher and learner; it guides the teacher to integrate text, graphics, animation, and other media into a multimedia instructional message that presents comprehensive information for her students (Mayer, 2005; Moreno & Mayer, 2007).

The classroom wherein multimedia learning informs instructional design and interactive learning provides students with an instructional message is necessary to achieve specified learning through both audio/verbal and visual modalities. Multimedia enables the demonstration of complicated processes in a highly interactive, animated fashion, such that instructional material can be interconnected with other related topics in a more natural and intuitive way (Frey & Sutton, 2010; Yamauchi, 2008).

The future classroom, using a teacher's instructional designs and presentations that embrace interactive multimedia learning, will be one in which the actions of the learner determine what happens in the learning experience. Simply stated, the defining feature of "interactivity is responsiveness to the learner's action during learning" (Moreno & Mayer, 2007, p. 311), whereas in a "non-interactive multimodal learning classroom, a multimedia message is presented in a pre-determined way irrespective of anything the learner does during learning" (p. 311).

As the digital generation enters the future classroom, it already has experienced interactivity in various forms in concert with media- and digital technologies-enriched learning.[4] Teachers advancing interactive multimedia instruction will draw on the digital generation's innate media and digital technologies skills and understanding to advance learning experiences that depend on the learner's actions during learning.[5]

In the future classroom, multimedia learning has the potential to encourage and enhance student learning, creativity, and innovation (Malik & Agarwal, 2012). Student success[6] in multimedia learning activities will occur as students interact meaningfully with their academic material, select relevant verbal and nonverbal information, organize information into corresponding mental models, and integrate new representations with existing knowledge when learning with multimedia (de Sousa, Richter, & Nel, 2017; Mayer, 2002).

FUTURE FORWARD

Future forward for education, multimedia and digital technologies, and multimedia and cognitive learning theories will have a significant impact on how we view and understand education overall, teaching and learning in particular, and life in the classroom for a new generation of students and teachers (Moreno & Mayer, 2007). Over the next decade, advanced multimedia and digital technologies will put education within the reach of many more individuals with specific learning needs and allow greater specialization in curriculum, instruction, and pedagogy than previously experienced.

With these benefits comes the challenge of ensuring that educator preparation programs and academic learning infrastructure are aligned with multimedia learning theory and guided by a commitment to meet the needs of a digital generation that enters classrooms with a rich experience in digital technologies. The preparation of teachers and leaders with the necessary level of skill and knowledge of multimedia learning theory in concert with experience in and understanding of multimedia and digital technologies is essential to transform school and university classrooms into interactive multimedia learning environments.

As we turn our attention to the needs of a digital generation entering classrooms, the realization is that teachers must not only know and understand the functions of multimedia and digital technologies available in a media- and technology-rich environment, but they also should know their responsibilities in terms of being multimedia and digital technology literate. As well, teachers will also require a fundamental working knowledge of multimedia learning theory and its implications for designing curriculum, instruction, and pedagogical strategies to engage the digital generation in learning.

Preparing a next generation of teachers to enter the classroom with an understanding of and appreciation for the digital generation's already advanced level of digital literacy and acumen for using digital technologies will require that teacher educators undergo a dramatic change in how learning is understood. Preparing teachers to take responsibility for multimedia-enriched instruction and curriculum in order to teach the digital generation will require that teacher educators understand a new paradigm of deep learning[7]—multimedia learning theory and cognitive load theory as a foundation for teaching and learning.

It is imperative to prepare a next generation of teachers who understand how to integrate multimedia learning and cognitive load theories into the daily activities of communicating, designing instruction, understanding the cognitive needs of students, and creating a learning space in classrooms that advances the learner as the center of everything consequential to teaching and learning of a digital generation. We must realize that the future classroom will be decidedly different each step forward, the demands constantly shifting with each new generation of students. The need will be pervasive to be in alignment with the advances in technological- and multimedia theory-based teaching and learning.

CONCLUSION

The rapid advancement of multiple forms of media and digital technologies in a Web 2.0—soon, Web 3.0—world requires a fundamental reorientation in our use of multimedia instructional strategies and learning theories as an infrastructure in educator preparation and practice. We will need to be selective and sophisticated in our decisions as to how we want to use media and digital technologies to learn and teach and inform the knowledge of each future generation of students.

The roles of both learner and teacher are changing, and will continue to change, in order to capitalize on the opportunities new technologies, the rapidly growing landscape of media, and the value of multimedia learning theory hold for education. The impact on our educational institutions will be enormous, and the transition to representing knowledge in various ways through multimedia and digital technologies will change the nature of our understanding of teaching and learning.

The ideal future will be one in which the roles of teacher, learner, and media and digital technologies are in balance and present an interactive learning space. The ideal future will be one where the advances in media and digital technologies in concert with changes in the internet and Web 2.0 are in synchronous motion with changes in teaching and learning, and vice versa. The ideal future will be one where teachers and learners are more concerned with the construction of knowledge than with mastery of all areas.

The teacher's role will be to design instructional messages that are multimodal in nature, focused on providing the learner with enriched learning experiences. These experiences will present a balance of forms of information (multimodal) with forms of delivery (multimedia) to ensure that learning is aligned with the cognitive needs of the learner. The teacher's role will be to challenge and stimulate the learner.

NOTES

1. Greer, Crutchfield, and Woods (2013) explain that multimedia learning "has its roots in the cognitive architecture that allows human learning to take place and the technological features that best support cognition" (p. 41).

2. Sweller (2005) explains that instructional design, as it relates to cognition and multimedia learning theory, "is driven by our knowledge of human cognitive structures and the manner in which those structures are organized" (p. 19).

3. Digital generation is used to designate those generations born from the 1980s onward and raised in a context where digital technologies form an inextricable part of daily life.

4. Davis (2008) is instructive on the value of interactive multimedia learning, noting that by using the multimedia technologies through the Web, the nature of interactivity and use of multiple media in learning enhance the students' learning process and provide a beneficial alternative to passive traditional learning.

5. Moreno and Mayer (2007) explain that the importance of a multimodal learning environment resides in the highly interactive nature of learning, "because rather than unilaterally presenting the verbal and non-verbal information needed to understand the process of photosynthesis, it allows for student input, different learning paces, and system feedback contingent on students' responses" (p. 312).

6. Researchers (Acuña & López-Aymes, 2016; Clark & Mayer, 2011; de Sousa, Richter, & Nel, 2017; Evans & Gibbons, 2007; Farias, Obilinovic, & Orrego, 2007; Greer, Crutchfield, & Woods, 2013; Mariano, 2014; McTigue, 2009; Moreno, 2007; Schrader, 2016; Yamauchi, 2008) provide evidence that students, both college age and younger, exhibit numerous and important differences when learning from multimedia content. Likewise, the studies indicate that student success in multimedia learning environments is increased. Important to note, in the Greer, Crutchfield, & Woods (2013) study, students with learning disabilities benefited from multimedia learning-enriched environments.

7. Moreno and Mayer (2007) explain that deep learning "depends on cognitive activity—such as selecting relevant information from a lesson, mentally organizing it into a coherent structure, and integrating the new knowledge with existing knowledge" (p. 312).

REFERENCES

Acuña, S. R., & López-Aymes, G. (2016). Collaborative multimedia learning: Influence of a social regulatory support on learning performance and on collaboration. *Journal of Curriculum and Teaching, 5*(2), 83–94.

Clark, R. C., & Mayer, R. E. (2011). *E-learning and the science of instruction: Proven guidelines for consumers and designers of multimedia learning* (3rd ed.). San Francisco, CA: Pfeiffer.

Davis, M. (2008). Classroom connections: Finding appropriate educational uses. *Education Week Digital Directions: Trends and Advice for k–12 Technology Leaders, 2*(Summer/Spring), 18–19. Retrieved from http://www.edweek.org/dd/articles/2008/06/09/01networks_side.h02.html.

Dawson, C. (2008). Web modules: Integrating curricula and technology standards. *AACE Journal, 16*(1), 3–20.

de Sousa, L., Richter, B., & Nel, C. (2017). The effect of multimedia use on the teaching and learning of social studies at tertiary level: A case study. *Yesterday & Today, 17*, 1–22. doi: http://dx.doi.org/10.17159/2223-0386/2017/n17a1.

Evans, C., & Gibbons, N. J. (2007). The interactivity effect in multimedia learning. *Computers & Education, 49*, 1147–1160.

Farias, M., Obilinovic, K., & Orrego, R. (2007). Implications of multimedia learning models on foreign language teaching and learning. *Columbian Applied Linguistics Journal, 9*, 174–199.

Frey, B. A., & Sutton, J. M. (2010). A model for developing multimedia learning projects. *MERLOT Journal of Online Learning and Teaching, 6*(2), 491–507.

Green, H., & Hannon, C. (2007). Their space: Education for a digital generation. Retrieved from http://www.demos.co.uk/files/Their%20space%20-%20web.pdf.

Greer, D. L., Crutchfield, S. A., & Woods, K. L. (2013). Cognitive theory of multimedia learning, instructional design principles, and students with learning disabilities in computer-based and online learning environments. *Technology in Education, 193*(2), 41–50.

Klopfer, E., Osterwell, S., Groff, J., & Haas, J. (2009). *Using the technology of today, in the classroom today: The instructional power of digital games, social networking, simulations, and how teachers can leverage them.* Boston, MA: Massachusetts Institute of Technology, The Education Arcade.

Malik, S. & Agarwal, A. (2012). Use of multimedia as a new educational technology tool—A study. *International Journal of Information and Education Technology, 2*(5), 468–471.

Mariano, G. (2014). Breaking it down: Knowledge transfer in a multimedia learning environment. *International Journal of Teaching and Learning in Higher Education, 26*(1), 1–11.

Mayer, R. E. (2002). Cognitive theory and the design of multimedia instruction: An example of the two-way street between cognition and instruction. *New Directions for Teaching and Learning, 89*, 55–71.

Mayer, R. E. (2005). Cognitive theory of multimedia learning. In R. E. Mayer (Ed.), *The Cambridge handbook of multimedia learning* (pp. 31–48). Cambridge, UK: Cambridge University Press.

McLuhan, M. (1964). *Understanding media: The extensions of man*. New York, NY: Mentor.

McTigue, E. M. (2009). Does multimedia learning theory extend to middle-school students? *Contemporary Educational Psychology, 34*, 143–153.

Moreno, R. (2007). Optimizing learning from animations by minimizing cognitive load: Cognitive and effective consequences of signaling and segmentation methods. *Applied Cognitive Psychology, 21*, 765–781.

Moreno, R., & Mayer, R. (2007). Interactive multimodal learning environments. *Educational Psychology Review, 19*, 309–326. doi: 10.1007/s10648-007-9047-2.

Schrader, P. G. (2016). Does multimedia theory apply to all students? The impact of multimedia presentations on science learning. *Journal of Learning and Teaching in Digital Age (JOLTIDA), 1*(1). Retrieved from http://www.joltida.org/index.php/joltida/rt/printerFriendly/8/90.

Sweller, J. (2005). The redundancy principle in multimedia learning. In R. E. Mayer (Ed.), *The Cambridge handbook of multimedia learning* (pp. 159–167). New York, NY: Cambridge University Press.

Yamauchi, L. G. (2008). Effects of multimedia instructional material on students' learning and their perceptions of the instruction. *Retrospective Theses and Dissertations*. 15324. Retrieved from https://lib.dr.iastate.edu/rtd/15324.

About the Contributors

Abbey N. Boorman is an independent consultant in education, providing services in K–12 educational technologies and literacy. In addition to professional coaching and teaching, Abbey has led workshops and presentations on integrating technology in the content areas and various topics in teaching reading and writing. As a teacher, she primarily worked with seventh and twelfth grade students in English language arts. In 2017, she was named Educator of the Year by Union Grove ISD. Abbey is passionate about working with children, integrating technology and multimedia in the classroom, and helping students prepare for an innovative future. She holds teaching certifications in English language arts and English as a second language, and she is a certified reading specialist and Google certified educator. Abbey is currently pursuing her EdD at Stephen F. Austin State University.

Charles L. Lowery is assistant professor at Ohio University where he teaches courses in the Department of Educational Studies and coordinates the educational administration program. He earned his EdD in educational leadership from Stephen F. Austin State University. In addition, he holds an MEd in educational administration and an MS in instructional design and technology. His major research interests include metaphors and mediated representations of school leadership and the concept of the scholar-practitioner educational leader as a moral democratic agent for justice, care, and critique.

Brooks Knight is a former high school mathematics and science teacher, campus administrator, and school district technology and instructional technology director in the Dallas area and East Texas. He holds a BBA in accounting, an MEd in secondary education, and an EdD in educational leadership. Brooks currently is a technology consultant for schools. As a teacher he was an early adopter of interactive whiteboards in the classroom. His doctoral dissertation focused on the theory of multimedia learning, with results illuminating additional variables that affect spatial reasoning. He has also trained teachers, administrators, and professors on technology use and often has conversations regarding expectations and reality behind how technology and the multimedia learning theory affect student memory and learning. He has found that it is impactful and important when administrators understand what should and likely should not be expected when implementing technology in the classroom. His mantra is, "If you think technology is the answer, you're likely asking the wrong question."

Richard E. Mayer is Distinguished Professor of Psychological and Brain Sciences at the University of California, Santa Barbara. His research interest is in applying the science of learning to education, with a focus on how to help people learn in ways that they can transfer what they have learned to new situations. His research is at the intersection of cognition, instruction, and technology, with current projects on multimedia learning, computer-supported learning, and computer games for learning. He served as president of Division 15 (educational psychology) of the American Psychological Association and vice president of the American Educational Research Association for Division C (learning and instruction).

He earned the E. L. Thorndike Award for career achievement in educational psychology, the Scribner Award for outstanding research in learning and instruction, the Jonassen Award for excellence in research in the field of instructional design and technology, the James McKeen Cattell Award for a lifetime of outstanding contributions to applied psychological research, and the American Psychological Association's Distinguished Contribution of Applications of Psychology to Education and Training Award. He was ranked the most productive educational psychologist in the world in *Contemporary Educational Psychology* and the most cited educational psychologist in Google Scholar.

He has served as principal investigator or co-PI on more than forty grants, including recent grants from the Office of Naval Research, the Institute of Education Sciences, and the National Science Foundation. He is former editor of the *Educational Psychologist* and former coeditor of *Instructional Science*, and he serves on the editorial boards of twelve journals, mainly in educational psychology. He is the author of more than five hundred publications including thirty books, such as: *Learning as a Generative Activity*; *Computer Games for Learning*; *Applying the Science of Learning*; *e-Learning and the Science of Instruction: Fourth Edition* (with R. Clark); *Multimedia Learning: Second*

Edition; *Learning and Instruction: Second Edition*; *Handbook of Research on Learning and Instruction: Second Edition* (coeditor with P. Alexander); and *The Cambridge Handbook of Multimedia Learning: Second Edition* (editor).

Scott McLeod, JD, PhD, is widely recognized as one of the nation's leading experts on K–12 school technology leadership issues. After fourteen years as an educational leadership professor, McLeod currently serves as director of learning, teaching, and innovation for Prairie Lakes Area Education Agency in Iowa. He also is the founding director of the UCEA Center for the Advanced Study of Technology Leadership in Education (CASTLE), the nation's only academic center dedicated to the technology needs of school administrators, and was a cocreator of the wildly popular video series *Did You Know? (Shift Happens)*.

He has received numerous national awards for his technology leadership work, including recognition from the cable industry, Phi Delta Kappa, the National School Boards Association, and the Center for Digital Education. In 2011 he was a Visiting Canterbury Fellow at the University of Canterbury in New Zealand. In 2013 he received the Technology Leadership Award for the state of Iowa. McLeod blogs regularly about technology leadership issues at *Dangerously Irrelevant* and is a frequent keynote speaker and workshop facilitator at national and international conferences. He also is coeditor of the book *What School Leaders Need to Know About Digital Technologies and Social Media*.

About the Editor

Patrick M. Jenlink is Regents Professor, the E. J. Campbell Endowed Chair; professor of educational leadership; professor of doctoral studies; and coordinator of the doctoral program in the Department of Secondary Education and Educational Leadership at Stephen F. Austin State University.

His experience as an educator includes: STEM teacher; building principal; school district superintendent; technology and computer applications professor at Northwestern Oklahoma State University; professor of computer and software applications at Western Michigan University; research consultant on NSF-funded Statewide Systemic STEM initiative in Michigan; and senior researcher on funded STEM initiatives in Oklahoma in conjunction with NASA and Oklahoma State University. He has written multiple grants in Oklahoma and Michigan for technology digital literacies innovation in K–12 schools with a focus on advancing educator knowledge and pedagogy.

Jenlink's research interests include media- and digital-based learning, multimodal literacies, meta-disciplinarity and pedagogy, educator preparation, and leadership for STEM innovation. His most recent book is *STEM Teaching: An Interdisciplinary Approach* (with Karen Embry Jenlink).

www.ingramcontent.com/pod-product-compliance
Lightning Source LLC
Chambersburg PA
CBHW022014300426
44117CB00005B/191